EXECUTIVE EDITORS
Sarah Galbraith, Alan Doan,
Jenny Doan, David Mifsud

MANAGING EDITOR
Natalie Earnheart

CREATIVE DIRECTOR
Christine Ricks

PHOTOGRAPHER
BPD Studios

CONTRIBUTING PHOTOGRAPHERS
Jake Doan, Katie Whitt

VIDEOGRAPHER
Jake Doan

DESIGNER & TECHNICAL WRITER
Linda Johnson

PROJECT DESIGN TEAM
Natalie Earnheart, Jenny Doan,
Sarah Galbraith

AUTHOR OF PATCHWORK MURDER
Steve Westover

CONTRIBUTING COPY WRITERS
Jenny Doan, Natalie Earnheart, Christine
Ricks, Katie Mifsud, Cammille Maddox,

COPY EDITOR
Geoff Openshaw

CONTRIBUTING PIECERS
Jenny Doan, Natalie Earnheart,
Kelly McKenzie, Cindy Morris, Carol
Henderson

CONTRIBUTING QUILTERS
Bernice Kelly, Deloris Burnett, Jamey Stone,
Betty Bates, Sherry Melton, Amber Weeks,
Sandi Gaunce, Daniela Kirk, Amy Gertz, Mari
Zullig, Megan Gilliam, Karen Russell, Kaitlyn
Adams, Mable Blanchard, Tia Gilliam, Isobel
Jensen, Linda Schwaninger, Debbie Allen

Cenveo Publisher Services
2901 Byrdhill Road
Richmond, VA 23228

CONTACT US
Missouri Star Quilt Company
114 N Davis
Hamilton, Mo. 64644
888-571-1122
info@missouriquiltco.com

6 COLOR CO-OP

16 SKATEBOARD

8 SAIL AWAY

32 PENNANT FLAGS

24 CRAZY BIRD

40 DRESSED TO THE NINES

content

FIRENZE 48

GOODNIGHT, IRENE 54

BEACH PICNIC 62

ORANGE PEEL 70

SANDY SUNRISE 78

JENNY'S CLASSROOM 86

HELLO
from MSQC

I was born near the sea and the ocean is an integral part of who I am. I love the undulating rhythm of the water. I love the sounds of the tide. I love the salty-fresh smell that isn't found anywhere else. I love the way the ocean constantly changes, and yet remains the same.

When the children were younger, one of our favorite songs to sing together went like this:

> Like a lighthouse standing bold against the gray,
> Shining through the night to warn of dangers in our way.
> Like a lighthouse, built on solid stone,
> Shedding light on weary seamen, who have drifted far from home.

Our family has been living smack dab in the middle of the United States for many years now, and though I am about as far from the ocean as a person can get, the Midwest has become as much a part of my identity as is the beautiful coast of California. After all, Missouri is where I discovered my passion for quilting, which has changed the course of my life forever!

I've found that even as you leave one home behind, there is always a new home - a new lighthouse - just waiting to be discovered. The ocean will always be close to my heart and I'm sure I will return many more times throughout my life, but my current home is what calls to me.

From the coast to the heartland, home is wherever you feel happy and at peace. The important thing is to take the time for those things that bring you joy. So take time to enjoy yourself this spring, wherever your home may be!

Jenny

JENNY DOAN
MISSOURI STAR QUILT CO

4

rainbows=spring

After a spring rain shower the air is fresh and everything seems new. The colors of the trees and flowers seem more vivid and bright. The smell of wet earth awakes my mind and makes my fingers want to go stick themselves into a pot of soil. Add a rainbow to this scene of a passing rain cloud and you have the makings of a perfect spring day.

Who doesn't love a rainbow? There's something about seeing a rainbow that renews my spirit and gives me a bright perspective. Why not make an invigorating new quilt with this rainbow of fabric! Adding rainbows and quilting together can only lead to a spry outlook on life and add a sunny spot to your day.

CHRISTINE RICKS
MSQC Creative Director, BLOCK MAGAZINE

SOLIDS

FBY8537 Cotton Supreme Solids - Redwork
by RJR Fabrics for RJR Fabrics
SKU: 9617-222

FBY8527 Cotton Supreme Solids - Mandarin
by RJR Fabrics for RJR Fabrics
SKU: 9617-159

FBY13016 Cotton Supreme Solids - Citron
by RJR Fabrics for RJR Fabrics
SKU: 9617-337

FBY12955 Cotton Supreme Solids - Sprout
by RJR Fabrics for RJR Fabrics
SKU: 9617-249

FBY8517 Cotton Supreme Solids - Royal Blue
by RJR Fabrics for RJR Fabrics
SKU: 9617-126

FBY12937 Cotton Supreme Solids - Amethyst
by RJR Fabrics for RJR Fabrics
SKU: 9617-215

PRINTS

FBY8582 Ziggy - Chevron Tomato
by French Bull for Windham Fabrics
SKU: 36536-1

FBY21976 Nomad - Adobe
by Urban Chiks for Moda Fabrics
SKU: 31106 13

FBY19533 Moxi - Floral Metro Spunky Sunny
by Studio M for Moda Fabrics
SKU: 32960 15

FBY19823 Quattro Piccolo - Fresh Grass
by Studio M for Moda Fabrics
SKU: 32985 45

FBY21595 Summer Celebration - Stars Blue
by Dani Mogstad for Riley Blake
C4444-BLUE

FBY16654 Cotton + Steel Basics Berry - Grapes Dottie
by Cotton + Steel for RJR Fabrics
SKU: 5002-010

sail
away

quilt designed by JENNY DOAN

Is there such a thing as a quilt without a story? So much time and care goes into making a quilt that by the time you put in the last stitch, that quilt already has quite a history. It's so fun to look at one of your quilts and have a whole flood of memories come rushing back.

One such memory involves this sailboat block. I once received a letter from a gal in England who wanted to surprise her mother with a birthday card from me. It was such a sweet gesture that I decided to send her a quilt block instead. After putting together a sailboat block, I sent it along with a note telling her that I wished I could sail across the ocean to wish her a happy birthday in person. Since then, this has become a favorite block of mine. It shares my love for the sea and brings other sweet memories to mind, one of which involves my very first sailing adventure in The Bahamas.

Raising our family on a tight budget, our vacations usually consisted of weekend camping trips or a visit to Grandma's house. We had wonderful times, of course, but I always dreamed of someday going on a real vacation to some exotic location.

For the tutorial and everything you need to make this quilt visit:
www.msqc.co/blockspring15

I finally got that chance a few years ago when my daughter Sarah and her husband Seth found an amazing deal on a trip to The Bahamas. The only catch was that we had to leave the very next day. . . so we did! Sarah, Seth, Ron, and I arrived in a land of amazing aqua blue water, and thus began a magical adventure that we will never forget!

One of the things we really wanted to do while we were there was sail a boat. It looked easy enough and we felt confident that we would be able to handle the boat on our own and sail elegantly through the tropical seas! It turns out we may have been slightly naive.

"Isn't it wonderful how many different stories one little quilt block can tell?"

We rented a boat and equipment from a man who gave us a few directions on how to sail and then promptly left to help other customers. So with zero experience and two-and-a-half minutes of instruction, we boarded our little boat and set sail. I found a comfy place to sit and happily hummed the tune from "Gilligan's Island" as Sarah, Seth, and Ron set to rigging up the sails. But, try as they might, we never got further than ten feet from shore! When frustration got the best of us, we threw in the towel and hired an experienced sailor so that we were able to sit back and enjoy the ride.

This Sailboat Quilt reminds me of that wonderful, haphazard trip to the Bahamas, my English quilting friend, and so many other fun times at sea. Isn't it wonderful how many different stories one little quilt block can tell?

materials

makes a 50½" X 53" quilt

QUILT TOP
- (1) 10" square pack print **OR**
    (12) 10" various print squares
- 1½ yds background solid

SASHING/BORDER/BINDING
- 1¾ yds coordinating fabric

BACKING
- 3¼ yds coordinating fabric

ADD'L MATERIALS
- MSQC 10" Half Hexagon Ruler

SAMPLE QUILT
- **Artisan Batiks Splendid 3** by Lunn Studios for Robert Kaufman
- **Kona Cotton White (1387)** by Robert Kaufman

1 boat shape

From the solid background yardage, cut (3) 10" WOF strips; subcut into (12) 10" squares.

Pair (1) solid & (1) print 10" square RST (12x). From each pair cut:
    (1) 5" x 10" rectangle pair
    (1) 5" x 5" square pair **1A**

Use the *MSQC Half Hexagon Ruler* to cut a "boat" shape from the 5" x 10" rectangle pair. **1B**

Cut *only* the *solid* half hexie shape in half again. **1C**

Sew each solid quarter to either side of

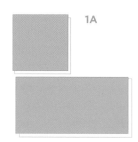
1A

1B

10" Half Hexagon Ruler

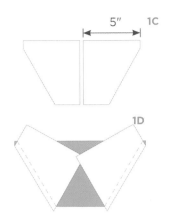

5"   **1C**

1D

the "boat." The placement can be tricky. Follow **1D**. This is the boat portion of the block. **1E** (12x)

2 set sail

Use (1) 5" x 5" pair (*cut above*) to make the sails. Sew ¼" around the perimeter of the pair. Cut across diagonally twice. **2A**

Yield: (4) HSTs.
Press to the print.

Arrange the (4) HSTs into the format shown. Sew blocks together side to side and then top to bottom as you would a 4-patch. Follow pressing arrows. **2B** Make 12 "sail" units.

Block size: 5¾" x 5¾"

3 build a ship

From the background solid yardage, cut (4) 4" WOF strips; subcut into (24) 5¾" rectangles.

Attach a background rectangle to either side of the sails.

Fingerpress a crease in the middle of the boat section along the top side. Match the center seam of the sail section to the crease. **3A** Sew the sails to boats—giving the boats sails in different prints.

Trim to: 12" x 9¾"

4 arrange

Lay out the blocks in a 3 x 4 setting in an eye-pleasing arrangement.

5 sashing

Measure the height of your ships to customize the sashing length.

From the sashing/border/binding fabric cut:
    (6) 2½" x WOF strips; subcut
    (3) strips into (12) 9¾" vertical
    sashing segments and set (3)
    WOF strips aside.

Add vertical sashing to blocks in odd rows on the right; in even rows on the left. Press to the sashing.

Sew blocks in rows together first, pressing seams to the sashing.

Measure & cut (3) horizontal sashing strips from the 2½" strips that were set aside. Ours was 41" long. Attach one to the bottom of all rows except the last one. Then, sew rows together.

Quilt Center Size: 41" x 43½"

1E

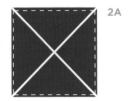

2A

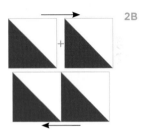

2B

3A

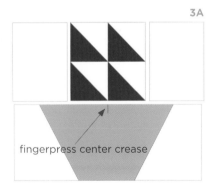

fingerpress center crease

4A

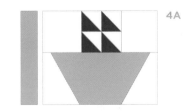

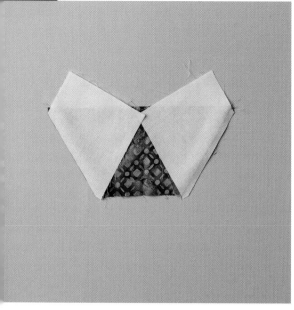

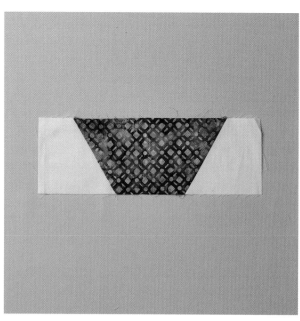

1   Sew a solid quarter hexie to either side of a print half hexie shape right sides together. This is how it should look. Step 1

2   This is the boat portion of the block. Step 1

3   Sew around the perimeter of a print + solid pair (cut from the 10" square). Then make 2 cuts on the diagonal. Step 2

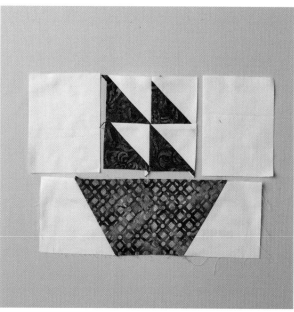

4   Arrange the (4) HSTs (half square triangles) to look like sails in the wind. Sew together as you would a 4-patch. Step 2

5   Add background rectangles to either side of the sails. Choose a boat of a different print and fold in half to mark its center with a fingerpressed crease. Step 3

6   Sew the sails to the boat, lining up their centers. Trim to 12" x 9¾." Step 3

6 borders

Cut (5) 5″ strips of outer border fabric. Follow steps in *construction basics* to attach to the quilt. Press to the borders.

7 quilt & bind

Layer quilt top on batting and backing and quilt the way you like. Square up all raw edges.

Cut (6) 2½″ strips from binding fabric to finish. See *construction basics* for greater detail.

skateboards

quilt designed by JENNY DOAN

Raising boys has been an adventure, to put it mildly.
We lived out on a farm when our boys were young, and
there's no better place for a little boy to grow up, with
the open country providing an endless number of places
to explore and be wild. Moving into town—even a small
town—was a big transition for them. For a while they
didn't know what to do with themselves in our newfound
metropolis, so they took up skateboarding.

I don't know if you've ever stepped on a skateboard
before, but I have, and I can tell you it is not easy! One
day the boys decided to drag me out skateboarding with
them, and ever since that near-death experience, I have
had a healthy respect for anyone who can stand up on a
skateboard, let alone do tricks.

The boys stuck with it and they actually got really good.
Every day they practiced on the front porch and gave
our retired neighbors some entertainment. It was a daily
ritual: the neighbors set up lawn chairs, muttered about
how those foolish kids were gonna break their necks,
and then sat back to watch the show.

*For the tutorial and everything
you need to make this quilt visit:*
www.msqc.co/blockspring15

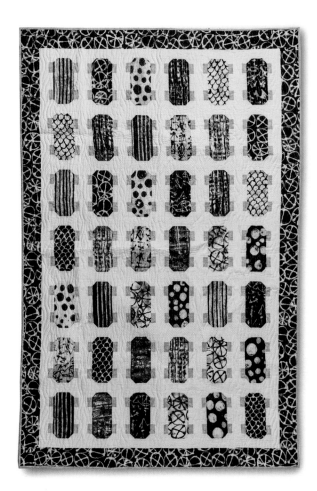

With an audience to please, the boys became increasingly adventurous. One day they got out their bikes and decided to make themselves a ramp. They moved our little car to the middle of the lawn and leaned a sheet of plywood up against it. They took turns riding down the driveway at breakneck speed until they hit the plywood and sailed up over the top of the car. I had no idea they were doing this until I happened to see one of them sail by the kitchen window. Talk about your heart skipping a beat!

The neighbors loved that one. One of them confided in me that having those young hooligans live across the street was the best entertainment they had had in years. Those boys were my best entertainment too. I'm just glad they lived to be adults!

"I don't know if you've ever stepped on a skateboard before, but I have, and I can tell you it is not easy!"

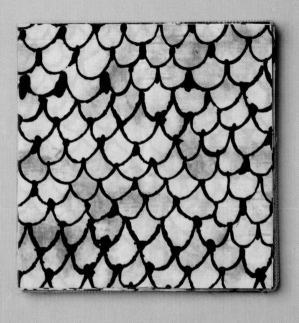

materials

makes a 61" X 90½" quilt

QUILT TOP
- (1) 10" square pack print *(enough for 2 quilts)*
- 2¾ yds background solid
- ½ yd green for wheels
- 1 yd outer border

BINDING
- ¾ yd coordinating fabric

BACKING
- 5½ yds **OR** 2¾ yds 90" wide

SAMPLE QUILT
- **Back & White** by Marcia Derse for Windham
- **Bella Solids White (98)** by Moda Fabrics
- **Handspray Jewel Box Lime Green (001)** by RJR

1 cut

Cut all 10" squares in half once. Use (42) 5" x 10" rectangles as skateboards.

From the background solid, cut:
- (12) 1½" WOF strips,
- (24) 2½" WOF strips, &
- (3) 4" WOF strips

2 skateboard

Cut (6) 1½" WOF strips into squares. Use the 1½" squares to snowball all 4 corners of the skateboards. Chain piecing will speed up this step. **2A**

Trim excess fabric and press the corners out. **2B**

2A

2B

3A

Subcut the strip sets into 1½" widths. These are the wheels.

Sew a wheel strip to either side of the skateboard. Press to the skateboard. **3B**

4 sashing +

Use (11) 2½" WOF background solid strips and subcut . . .

  into 2½" x 10" segments.

Add a 2½" x 10" background segment to the right side of each skateboard block. **4A**

Skateboard size: 9" x 10"

5 arrange

Lay the skateboards out in a 6 x 7 setting. Sew them together side-to-side in rows across. Press to the sashing. **5A**

Sew the remaining (13) 2½" WOF strips of background fabric together end-to-end and subcut into (8) 51" segments.

Average the width of your actual rows for the best results.

Attach a strip to the bottom of each row, and add one to the top of the first row as well. Press to the sashing.

Sew rows together to build the quilt center.

Measure the quilt length and add a last strip to the quilt's left side. Press to the sashings. **5B**

Quilt Center Size: 53½" x 83"

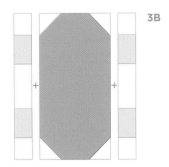

3B

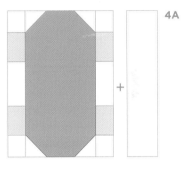

4A

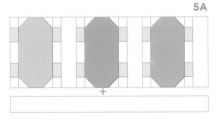

5A

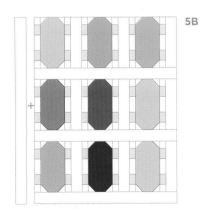

5B

3 wheels

Use (6) 1½" and (3) 4" WOF background solid strips. In addition . . . from the green fabric, cut:

  (6) 2½" WOF strips

Sew 5 strips together lengthwise in this order to make a strip set: **3A**

  1½" background strip
  2½" green strip
  4" background strip
  2½" green strip
  1½" background strip

To avoid "rainbowing" the strips, alternate sewing directions from strip to strip. Press seams gently to the green fabric.

Make (3) strip sets.

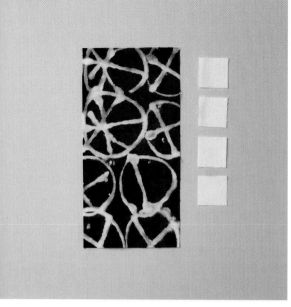

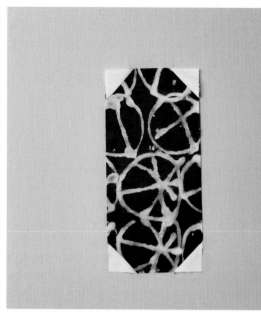

1   To build the skateboard, use (1) 5″ x 10″ rectangle and (4) 1½″ solid squares. Step 2

2   Set the squares on every corner of the skateboard and sew across them on the diagonal. Step 2

3   Trim the excess fabric and press the corners out. Step 2

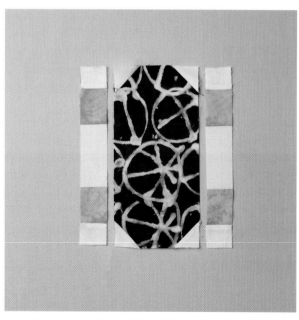

4   Cross cut the strip sets into 1½″ wheel sets. You'll need 2 for each skateboard. Step 3

5   Add a 2½″ x 10″ sashing segment to the right side of each skateboard. Step 4

A

C

D

B

Average the width of your actual rows for the best results.

Attach a strip to the bottom of each row, and add one to the top of the first row as well. Press to the sashing.

Sew rows together to build the quilt center.

Measure the quilt length and add a last strip to the quilt's left side. Press to the sashings. **5B**

Quilt Center Size: 53½" x 83"

6 outer border

Cut (8) 4" strips of outer border fabric. Follow steps in *construction basics* to attach to the quilt. Press to the borders.

7 quilt & bind

Layer quilt top on batting and backing and quilt the way you like. Square up all raw edges.

Cut (8) 2½" strips from binding fabric to finish. See *construction basics* for greater detail.

crazy *birds*

designed by JENNY DOAN

When our son Alan was very young, three or four years old, he took it upon himself to be our resident seagull chaser. He saw himself as a superhero, coming to the rescue of beach picnics everywhere. At times I cringed when he came barrelling down the beach, arms over his head, shouting at the top of his lungs at a seagull who had come too close, never noticing the unsuspecting sunbathers he sprayed with sand as he ran. But I have to admit, I appreciated his pest control skills. Seagulls are crazy! They'll do anything to snatch a crumb.

We have our own crazy bird here at MSQC—crazy, but far more welcome than those pesky seagulls. In fact, Alan (now all grown up of course) picked it out himself! People ask me where that

For the tutorial and everything you need to make this quilt visit:
www.msqc.co/blockspring15

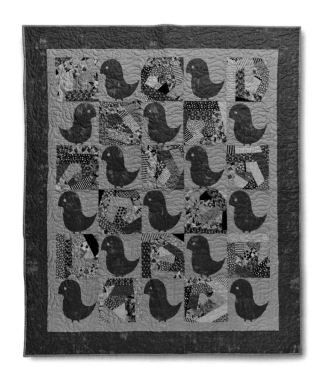

crazy bird quilt

random duck in all of our quilting tutorials came from, but if you take a closer look you'll see that's no duck. It's actually a chick that quacks! Who knows why, but I love it. Our little Missouri Star chick has become an important part of the MSQC family.

I asked Alan to help me figure out how to get a quacking ring tone, or make the shop door quack when it opens, but he just said I'd stand there all day opening the door to make it quack. And I guess he's right. They say motherhood is like being

pecked to death by a duck: ducklings keep on poking at you, but they never break the skin. I raised seven kids and I can tell you that makes a lot of sense to me. I guess that's why I love that weird little quacking chick. Maybe we're both a little nuts!

"We have our own crazy bird here at MSQC—crazy, but far more welcome than those pesky seagulls."

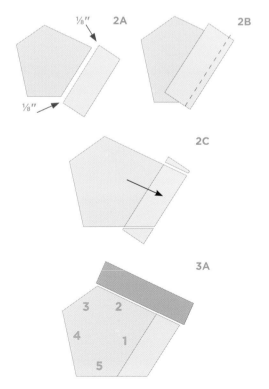

materials

makes a 61½" X 71" quilt

QUILT TOP
- (1) 2½" WOF roll print
- (1) 10" square pack solid **OR**
  1¼ yds background solid fabric
- 1¼ yds for crazy birds
- ½ yd inner border solid (same as bknd solid)
- 1 yd outer border

BINDING
- ½ yd coordinating fabric

BACKING
- 4 yds coordinating fabric

ADD'L MATERIALS
- 2¼ yds 18" wide Heat 'n Bond

SAMPLE QUILT
- **Gardenvale** by Jen Kingswell for Moda Fabrics
- **Kona Cotton Ash (1007)** by Robert Kaufman
- **Pink Grunge** by Moda Fabrics

The following materials are optional:
- MSQC 4" Crazy Block Ruler
- MSQC 10" Square Ruler
- MSQC "Bird" Die Cut #659796 by Sizzix

1 cut

Cut out (15) crazy block shapes from various 2½" WOF strips. Use the diagram provided or the *MSQC 4" Crazy Block Ruler*.

2 build the block

Pick any side of the center shape to start on. Cut a strip to that length plus at least ¼"—or ⅛" beyond each edge. **2A**

Sew the strip to the center shape right sides together (RST) with a ¼" seam. **2B**

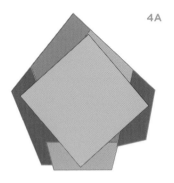

4A

4B

5A

wrong side

5B

Press to the strip. Trim the strip ends even with the adjacent sides. 2C

3 additional strips

Move around the crazy quilt center adding various strips. Choose a direction to move around the center and stick with it—be consistent. 3A Trim after attaching each strip.

Note: Keep checking the block size as you near a 10″ square. You may only need partial strips to cover final areas.

Stop when you have a fabric piece that is larger than 10″ square.

4 square it up

Use the MSQC 10″ Square Ruler to trim to size. Make 15. 4A

Block size: 10″ x 10″ 4B

5 crazy bird block

From the crazy bird fabric, cut (4) 10″ WOF strips; subcut into (15) 10″ squares. Repeat with the background fabric.

Adhere a 9″ x 9½″ rectangle of *Heat 'n Bond* to the wrong side of each crazy bird fabric square.

Use the Sizzix die cut to make crazy birds, or trace the shape onto the Heat 'n Bond side with the template provided. Flip one bird so that it will face the opposite direction. 5A Cut out birds, including the bird's eye.

Center the birds on 10″ background solid squares and fuse into place. Using a zig-zag, blanket or decorative stitch, sew around the bird's silhouette. 5B

6 arrange

Lay the blocks into a 5 x 6 setting, alternating crazy blocks and birds both across in rows, and down in columns. Position the "crazy bird" facing the wrong direction.

Sew blocks together in rows, side-to-side. Press to the bird blocks. Sew rows together & nest seams.

Quilt Center Size: 48″ x 57½″

7 borders

From the inner border fabric cut (6) 2½″ WOF strips. Follow steps in *construction basics* to attach to the quilt. A-D Press to the borders.

Cut (7) 5″ WOF strips of outer border fabric. Attach to the quilt in the same manner as the inner border.

8 quilt & bind

Layer quilt top on batting and backing and quilt the way you like. Square up all raw edges.

Cut (7) 2½″ WOF strips from binding fabric to finish. See *construction basics* for greater detail.

1 The crazy quilt center can easily be cut from a 2½″ strip. Step 1

2 Right sides together (RST), attach a second strip to one side of the crazy center. Each strip should be at least ¼″ longer than the side's length. Step 2

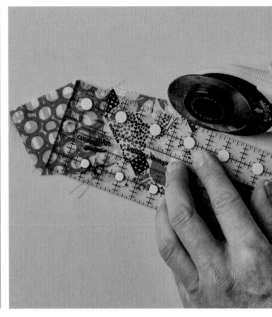

3 Trim the strip even with the adjacent sides of the crazy center. Step 2

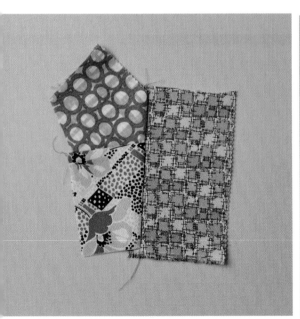

4 Add the next strip in a counterclockwise direction, always crossing the seam just sewn. Step 2

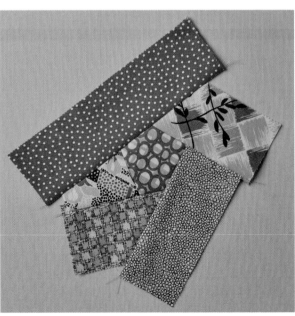

5 Continue to build the block until it measures more than 10.″ Step 3

6 Square up the block to 10.″

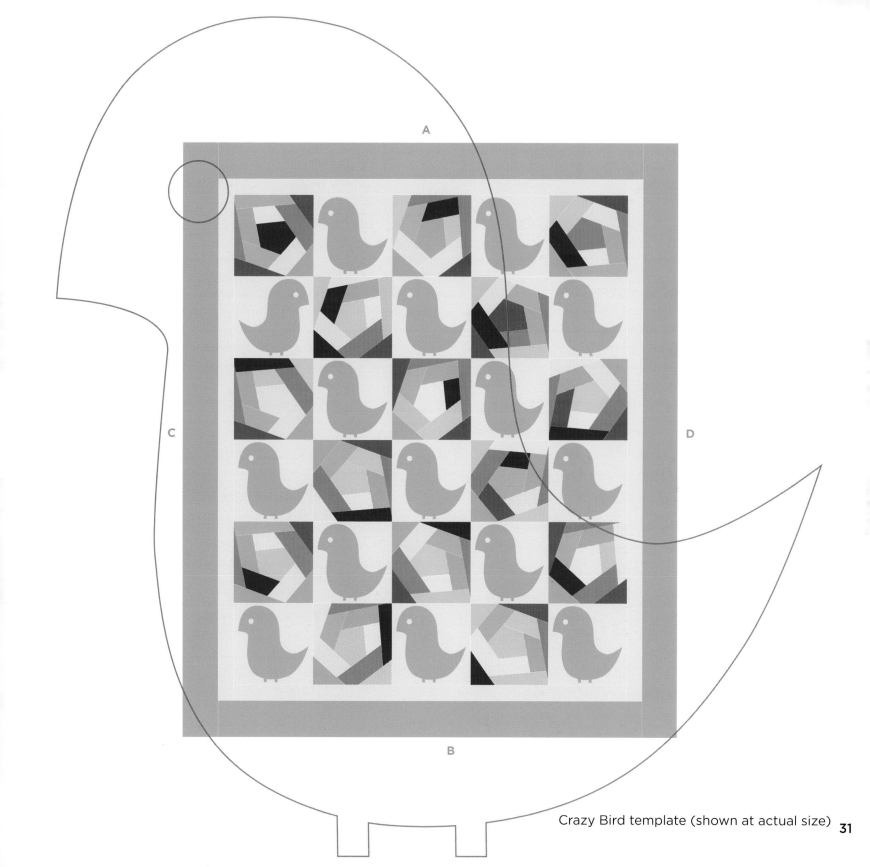

Crazy Bird template (shown at actual size)

pennant
flags

designed by JENNY DOAN

My maternal grandparents are Swedish immigrants, and when my mother was a child she loved listening to stories they told of growing up by the sea in Sweden. My Mormor (Swedish for mother's mother) often spoke of taking lunch to her father when she was a little girl. Her father worked on a ship with many flags on the masts and lines. Though many of the details of her childhood had faded from memory by the time she was older, she vividly remembered those big ships with the sails and pennant flags flapping in the wind. Every day she walked down a hill to the docks carrying her father's lunch in a metal pail and every day those flags were there.

My mother always dreamed of visiting Sweden to see with her own eyes the places that she had known her whole life through the stories of her parents. Her wish came true a few years ago when my sister Melissa

For the tutorial and everything you need to make this quilt visit:
www.msqc.co/blockspring15

orchestrated a trip for as many of us as could tag along.

It's funny how you can feel so connected to a place that you have never before visited. The instant we set foot on Swedish soil, we felt a bit like we had come home. My mom is very involved in genealogy and has maintained relationships with distant family members who still live in Sweden, and many of them were there to greet us when we arrived.

This wonderful vacation was full of fun memories and new adventures, but the highlight of the trip was when we visited the very house that Mormor had lived in when she was small. Mom was elated to see it and wanted her picture taken in front of the home. She walked up to the doorway and as she turned around to smile for the camera she looked down the hill, and there at the water's edge was a large ship that was decorated in a wonderful criss-cross of pennants.

Mom stood there in amazement and drank in the moment. We later learned that the ship

was definitely not the ship on which my great grandfather had worked; it was a Russian clipper that was docking for a race. But as my mother stood on the very spot where Mormor had lived so many years ago, I know that in her mind's eye she could see a little girl skipping down the street, pail in hand.

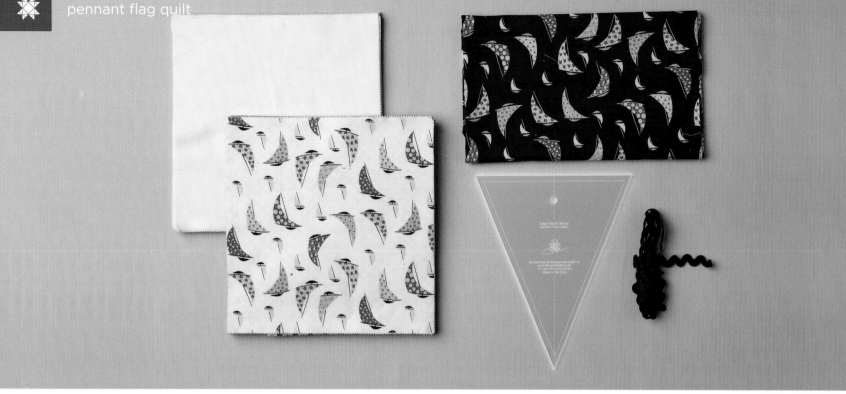

materials

makes a 64¼" X 84" quilt

QUILT TOP
- (1) 10" square pack print
  (enough for 2 quilts)
- 3¼ yds background solid
- 1 yd outer border

BINDING
- ¾ yd coordinating fabric

BACKING
- 5 yds **OR** 2 yds 90" wide

ADD'L MATERIALS
- MSQC Large Simple Wedge
- 9½ yds ¾" Rickrack

SAMPLE QUILT
- **Daysail** by Bonnie & Camille for
  Moda Fabrics
- **Bella Solids White (98)** by Moda Fabrics

1 cut

Cut (2) *MSQC Large Simple Wedge*
shapes from each 10" print square. **1A**
Select (42) wedges.

From the solid background fabric cut
(5) 9⅛" WOF strips; subcut into wedges,
flipping the ruler as you go. **1B**

Yield: 10 per strip.

Make 2 stacks of wedges—prints &
solids—all prints pointing down, all
solids pointing up.

1A

1B

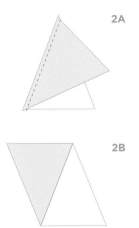

2A

2B

2 sew

Keep the wedges' orientation and pair them consistently with the print to the same side. 2A

RST, chain piece all pairs. Snip apart, and press to the print. You now have pennant pairs. 2B

3 arrange & trim

Lay out the pennant pairs in 6 rows of 7 print pennants each.

Sew the pairs together in rows. Add a final solid pennant to the last print pennant of each row. 3A

Next, straighten each end of all rows. Match the wedge ruler to the solid pennant, then swing the ruler's bottom edge out until the dotted center line aligns with the outside edge. 3B Keeping the top

points matched, cut the pennant down the middle. 3C

Row size: 47¾" x 8¾"

4 sashing

Always press seams to the sashing.
From the background solid fabric, cut (13) 4" WOF strips.

Sew (9) of these end to end in one long strip. Subcut into (7) 47¾" lengths (number of rows).
Note: Adjust this measurement to the average length of your pennant rows.

Attach a sashing strip to the bottom of every row. 4A Then sew rows together. Add the last strip to the top of the quilt.

Piece together the remaining (4) 4" strips end-to-end. Cut (2) 74½" lengths and attach to either side. 4B *Measure your quilt top length before cutting.*

Quilt Center size: 54¾" x 74½"

5 rickrack trim

Measure the width of the quilt. Add about an inch and cut rickrack trim to that size. You'll need one for each row of pennants, i.e. (6) 56."

Attach just above the pennants by stitching down the center of the rickrack with a zig-zag stitch. The ends of the rickrack trim will be captured in the side seams when the outer border is added. 5A

3A

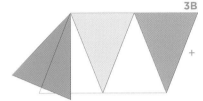

3B

3C

4A

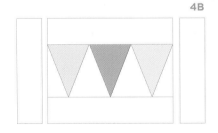

4B

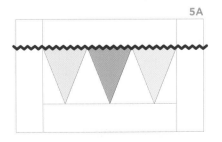

5A

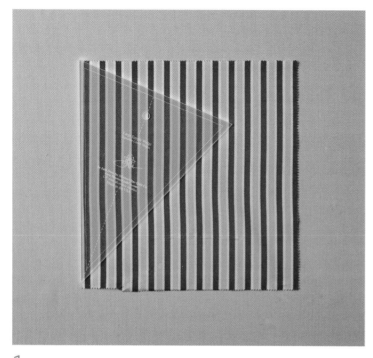

1 2 wedges can be cut from each 10″ square. Step 1

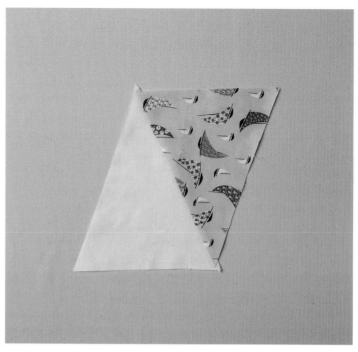

2 Be consistent. If you add a print wedge to the right side, continue in this fashion. Step 2

3 Notice the solid wedge top point is paired to the print wedge's wider edge. Step 2

4 Once a row is complete, trim the solid wedges on the ends. Step 3

6 borders

From the outer border fabric cut (7) 5″ strips. Follow steps in *construction basics* to attach to the quilt. **A-D** Press to the borders.

7 quilt & bind

Layer quilt top on batting and backing and quilt the way you like. Square up all raw edges.

Cut (8) 2½″ strips from binding fabric to finish. See *construction basics* for greater detail.

*For the tutorial and everything
you need to make this quilt visit:*

www.msqc.co/blockspring15

dressed
to the
nines

designed by JENNY DOAN

Next to the queen, the princess rules. We had three little girls in a row, and they were all princesses. Now my children have grown up to have their own share of princesses. In fact, ten of our grandchildren are girls. We Doans know about princesses.

But in all my years dealing with girls I have to say that the girliest, most princessy little girl of all was my granddaughter Jenna.

Jenna inherited an independent spirit from her mother. My daughter Natalie learned early on to pick her battles, and one of the battles she chose to not fight was clothing. Jenna was pretty much given free rein over what she wore, and nine times out of ten she was in a princess dress.

One year for her birthday I gave Jenna an assortment of plastic dress up shoes. Jenna squealed with delight, but Natalie just rolled her eyes. She knew right away those shoes would not be worn only at dress up time.

It didn't matter if she was going to preschool or the grocery store, Jenna was always decked out in full royal attire: gown, tiara, and those little plastic heels that

always went "CLICK, CLACK, CLICK, CLACK" with every tiny step.

Jenna was so dedicated to her princess style that she even dressed up when she was sick. When most kids stay home from school with a cold or the flu, they lounge about the house in pajamas or sweats. Not Jenna. Jenna could have a fever and still be dressed to the nines. She'd lie on her mom's bed cuddled up with a feather boa around her neck and a plastic cocktail ring on every finger.

But as with all princesses, Jenna eventually grew up and traded in her fairytale clothes for teenage fashions. Looking back, I'm so glad Natalie had the wisdom to allow Jenna to live her young life as a princess. Our little girls grow up so quickly and much too often they forget how fabulous they really are. So treasure your little princesses and enjoy those few precious years when "Happily Ever After" happens every single day!

"... treasure your little princesses and enjoy those few precious years when "Happily Ever After" happens every single day!"

materials

makes a 68" X 94" quilt

QUILT TOP
- (5) 5" square packs print
- ½ yd accent fabric
- ½ yd inner border
- 1½ yds outer border

BINDING
- ¾ yd coordinating fabric

BACKING
- 5¾ yds 44" **OR** 3 yds 90" wide

SAMPLE QUILT
- **Princess Life** by Robert Kaufman

1 cut

From the accent fabric, cut (3) 5" WOF strips; subcut into (24) 5" squares.

2 build the block

Select (8) 5" print squares to use with (1) 5" accent square.

Layout the squares in a 9-patch setting (3 x 3). Position the accent square in the middle. **2A**

Sew the blocks together in rows pressing seams according to the arrows. Then sew rows together. **2B**

Make (24) 9-patch blocks

Block Size: 14" x 14"

3 cut it up

Make (2) centered cuts through the block, one horizontal, the other vertical. Each quarter-block will have a small accent square in one corner. **3A**

4 reconstruct

Randomly select (4) quarter blocks to reconstruct into one block.

Lay these in a 2 x 2 setting, turning the accent squares so that (2) are facing across from each other in the center; and (2) are located at opposite corners on the outside perimeter. **4A**

Sew together as you would a 4-patch: top and bottom pairs, pressing seams in opposite directions to better nest them.

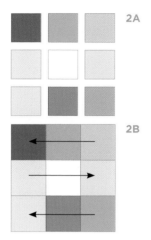

2A

2B

 Tip *Focus fabrics placed in the corners will ensure they remain large squares.*

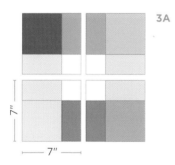

3A

7"

7"

Then sew top & bottom rows to each other. Do not press the last seam at this time. **4B**

Place a pin in the top center. This is right side up.

Block size: 13½" x 13½"

5 quilt center

Lay the blocks out into a 4 x 6 setting, either right side up, or upside down. Pins will *not* be sideways. **5A**

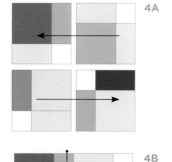

4A

4B

 Tip *All blocks will have the same configuration whether they are upside down or right side up.*

column 1   column 2

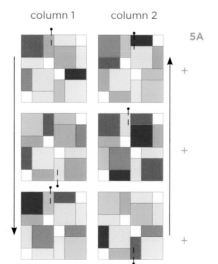

5A

+

+

+

+   +

Once you are pleased with the arrangement, press the last horizontal seams of the blocks down in odd columns; up in even columns.

Sew blocks together in columns first. Press seams according to which column they are in, even or odd. Then sew columns together, nesting seams as you go.

Press seams to one side.

Quilt Center size: 52½" x 78½"

6 borders

From the inner border fabric cut (7) 2½" WOF strips. Follow steps in *construction basics* to attach to the quilt. **A-D** Press to the borders.

Cut (8) 6" WOF strips of outer border fabric. Attach to the quilt in the same manner as the inner border.

7 quilt & bind

Layer quilt top on batting and backing and quilt the way you like. Square up all raw edges.

Cut (9) 2½" WOF strips from binding fabric to finish. See *construction basics* for greater detail.

45

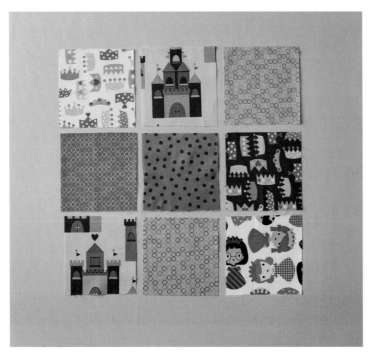

1 Arrange (8) 5″ squares around a center 5″ accent square in a 3 x 3 setting. If you want focus fabrics to remain whole squares, set them to the outside corners. Step 2

2 Sew the squares together across in rows first; then sew the rows to each other. Press seams in opposite directions from row to row to help with nesting seams. Step 2

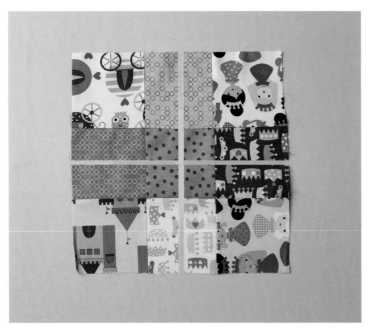

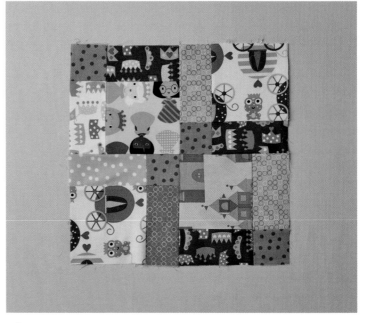

3 Cut the 9-patch in half once horizontally and once vertically. Note that each quarter-block has a small accent square in one corner. Step 3

4 Select (4) quarter blocks randomly to reassemble as one block. Notice the 2 accent squares touching in the center and 2 others located at opposite corners. Construct all the blocks exactly in the same manner. Step 4

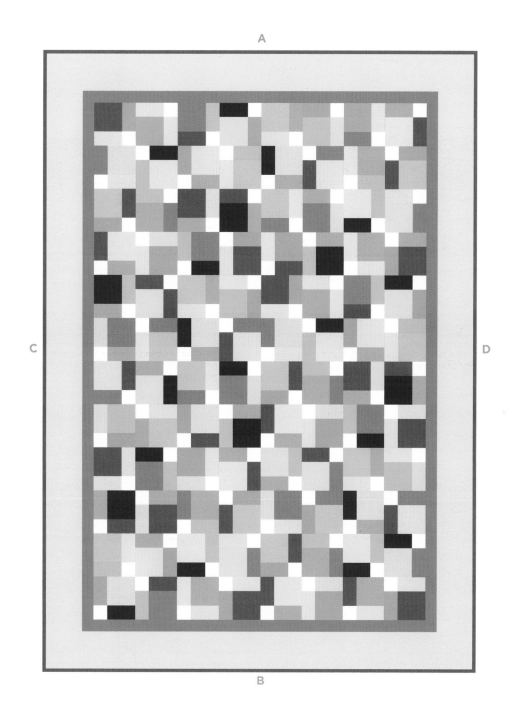

A

B

C

D

For the tutorial and everything you need to make this quilt visit:
www.msqc.co/blockspring15

firenze quilt

quilt designed by SHANNON FABRICS

Having grown up around the water in California, our family developed a real love for the ocean. Of course, out here in Missouri we're about as far from the coast as you can get. We love our Midwestern home, but every so often our hearts still long for the sea.

A few years ago, my daughter Sarah decided she wanted to share her love of the ocean with her children. She ached to have the kids' eyes fill with wonder when they saw the endless expanse of Pacific blue for the very first time. She had visions of the little ones building grand sand castles and of the teenagers coasting over the surf on boogie boards. So, they packed up the car and headed west.

Traveling across the United States with five small children ages five to sixteen is no small undertaking. The family drove for days and though the kids got restless, but Sarah knew that it would all be worth it in the end.

"There truly is no place like home. Ocean or desert, mountain or plain, we tend to love what we know."

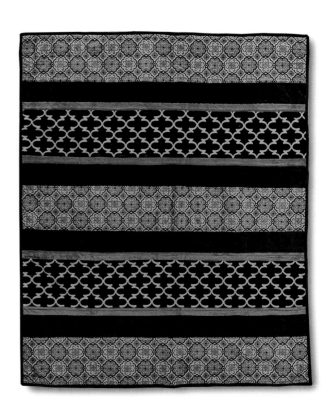

When they finally arrived, Sarah could hardly contain her excitement. She led her children down to where the sand meets the water and then stood back, waiting for their reactions. And the kids did like it. Really, they did. It was nice and pretty and fun—for a few minutes. Then the complaints began: "I'm cold!" "It's too windy here!" "I'm getting sand in my shoes!"

They piled back into the car and drove up to the next beach, and then the next. Finally, six-year-old Jason groaned in an exasperated little voice, "Can we just agree that all the water touches all the sand so all the beaches are the same?" Everyone laughed, but Sarah couldn't help but feel a little stab of disappointment.

An important lesson was learned that day. There truly is no place like home. Ocean or desert, mountain or plain, we tend to love what we know. Oh, it's fun to venture off to faraway lands and see new sights, but in the end we all long for that place where we feel most comfortable—that place where familiar landscapes and friendly faces combine to create that magical place we call home.

materials

makes a 60" X 68" quilt

QUILT TOP

All fabrics 60" wide
- 1 yd Green Tile
- ⅔ yd Navy Tile
- 1 yd Navy Solid
- ⅓ yd Teal Solid

BACKING
- 2 yds coordinating fabric

ADDITIONAL MATERIALS
- 505 Quilt Basting Spray
- Batting 60" x 78"

SAMPLE QUILT
- **Bella Vita** by Shannon Fabrics

1 cut

Cut fabrics into 60" WOF strips as follows:

Green Tile:	(3) 10" strips
Navy Tile:	(2) 10" strips
Navy solid:	(4) 5" &
(binding)	(5) 2" strips
Teal solid:	(4) 2½" strips

2 prepare

Lay the backing on a flat surface wrong side up. Position the batting squarely on top. Smooth out the surface. Lift half the batting back and spray 505 adhesive to its surface. Reposition the backing and repeat with the other half.

Mark the horizontal center of the batting/backing unit. **2A** Use 505 to adhere a 10" green tile strip right side up on the center line.

3 sew

Working from the center strip out, place a 5" navy solid strip RST along one edge of the green tile strip. Pin to hold. Use a ½" seam allowance throughout. Sew the strips together through all layers, batting and backing included. **3A**

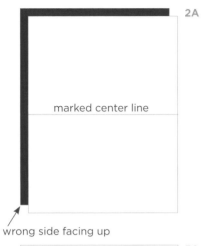

2A

marked center line

wrong side facing up

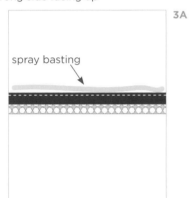

3A

spray basting

4 10" navy tile
5 2½" teal
6 5" navy solid
7 10" green tile

4 finishing

Trim & square up. Sew a running stitch around the quilt's perimeter.

Sew the (5) 2" navy solid strips together

with diagonal seams into one long strip. Join the ends with a diagonal seam.

Because the fabric does not ravel, complete the quilt with a raw edged finish. Bring the single layer binding around to the front and topstitch down with a zig-zag or decorative stitch—no need to fold the binding under!

Spray adhesive on the batting behind the second strip and smooth the strip into place.

Repeat with another 5" navy solid strip on the opposite side of the green tile fabric.

Except for the first strip, always add strips in pairs—first on one side, then on the other—working from the center out in the following order: 3B

1 10" green tile (center)
2 5" navy solid
3 2½" teal

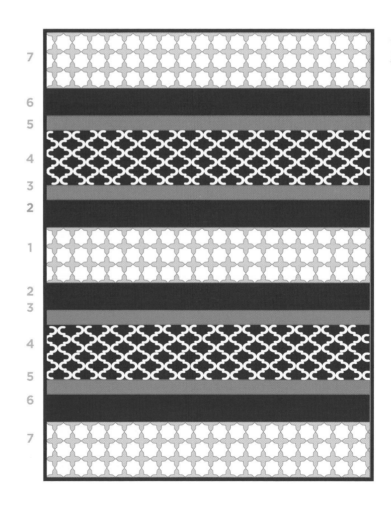

goodnight, irene

designed by JENNY DOAN

There's something about an old love story that gets me every time. Somehow it seems like life was a little more romantic in the days before selfies, social media, and texting, when a man asked a girl out properly and wore a suit when he picked her up. Even the love songs of the past were better. What woman can listen to "Unforgettable," "Five Minutes More," or "Only You" without melting a little?

Back in those dreamier days, my husband's mother was a young woman just starting out on her own. Her name was Mamie Irene Crisp, but she went by her middle name, Irene. She was born on April 8th 1923 in Prairie Grove, Arkansas. When she was about twenty, she followed her sister Reba and her father Jim to Salinas, California, where she found work in the lettuce sheds. Many a night she walked to Market Street to go dancing,

For the tutorial and everything
you need to make this quilt visit:
www.msqc.co/blockspring15

and it was there she met the love of her life, Desmond Henry Doan, also known as Jack. Jack was a member of the Coast Guard stationed in California at that time. Grandma loved a man in uniform, and when Jack saw her dance moves, he was had!

Irene and Jack fell for each other pretty quickly. Eventually, Jack's service obligation was over and after he went to San Francisco to muster out, he and Irene got married on January 12, 1945. They had three children and were married for over fifty-five years.

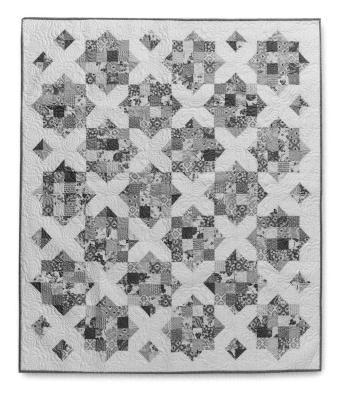

One of my favorite memories of Jack involves him and his brothers. Whenever he and his passel of brothers got together, they sang "Goodnight Irene" to Jack's sweet wife before the night ended. I've seen it myself and it's a sight to see, everyone singing while Irene beams with a huge smile on her face and a blush on her cheeks.

Jack and Irene have both passed on, but I'll bet somewhere out there a couple in love is still dancing to "Goodnight Irene."

materials
makes a 57" X 65" quilt

QUILT TOP
- (4) 5" square packs print
- (3) 5" square packs solid + ¼ yd
  OR 2¼ yds solid

BINDING
- ½ yd coordinating fabric

BACKING
- 3¾ yds coordinating fabric

SAMPLE QUILT
- **Floribella** by Emily Taylor for Riley Blake
- **Cotton Supreme Optical White (59)** by RJR

1 4-patch blocks

Select (2) 5" squares to pair RST.
Sew 2 seams on opposite edges. **1A**

Cut the pair in half between the two
seams at 2½." Press to the dark side.
1B

Repeat for a total of (42) pairs.

Match 2 random pairs RST, nesting
seams. Sew them together crossing
the seams. Continue adding pairs in
this fashion creating one long strip.
1C *No need to press yet.*

Starting at the far left, fold the first

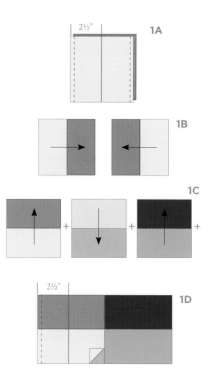

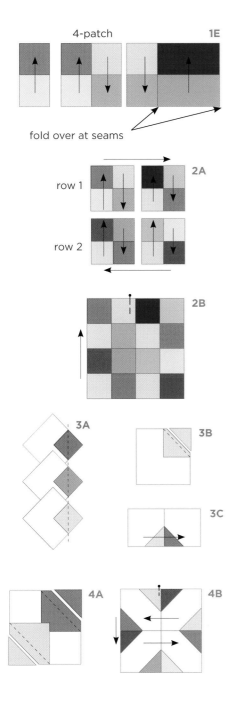

4-patch

1E

fold over at seams

row 1

2A

row 2

2B

3A

3B

3C

4A

4B

block over on top of the second RST. Cut at 2½." **1D**

You will have a 4-patch block. Set the half-block aside. Continue folding and cutting through the entire length of blocks. **1E** Finally, sew the remaining half-blocks together.

Yield: (84) 4-patch blocks.

2 build 16-patch

Select (4) random 4-patch blocks. Lay them into a 2 x 2 grid. Keep the last seam sewn in a vertical orientation. This will facilitate nesting seams and help make more precise intersections.

Sew blocks in row 1 together nesting seams. Do the same for row 2. *Now press all vertical seams in each row according to the long pressing arrows.* **2A**

Place a pin at the top of the block. Press the final seam toward the pin. **2B** Make (21) 16-patch blocks & set aside.

Block size: 8½" x 8½"

3 snowball it!

Cut (55) 5" print squares in half vertically and horizontally to yield (4) 2½" squares from each.

Trim all solid squares to 4½"—and/or cut 4½" squares from yardage. Set (4) aside for border corners.

To snowball the solid blocks, lay a 2½" print square on a solid 4½" square's corner RST. Sew across the print square on the diagonal. Chain piece the blocks, feeding one pair after another through the machine. **3A** Snip apart and trim the excess fabric. *Do not press yet.* **3B**

Select (2) blocks and lay them side-to-side, matching their snowballed corners. Press seams in the same direction and sew together. Make (26) of these snowballed pairs. These are the pieced border blocks. Set aside. **3C**

4 X-blocks

With the remaining blocks, snowball a second corner opposite the first, chain piecing the blocks again. Separate and trim the corner. **4A**

Block size: 4½" x 4½"

Select (4) snowballed blocks and arrange them in a 2 x 2 grid. *Before sewing,* press all seams in the top row to the left; all seams in the bottom row to the right. Sew together like a 4-patch—rows first, pressing seams according to arrows; then rows to each other. **4B**

Place a pin at the top. Press the final seam down. Make (21) X-blocks.

Block size: 8½" x 8½"

1 Nest seams from one block to the next as you sew them together in one long strip. Step 1

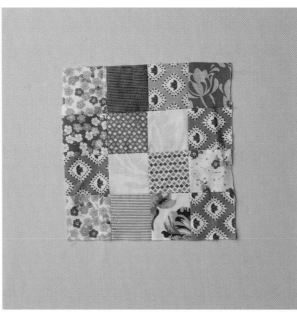

2 Select (4) random 4-patch blocks and assemble them into a single 16-patch. Step 2

3 Snowball opposite corners of a solid 4½" square with (2) 2½" print squares to make an X-block. Sew across the print squares on the diagonal. Step 3

4 A 4½" snowballed solid square is ¼ of an X-block. Step 4

5 Randomly select (4) snowballed squares to make an X-block. Sew together as you would a 4-patch. Note the pressing arrows. Step 4

6 Alternate X-blocks and 16-patches both across in rows and down in columns to lay out the quilt center. Step 5

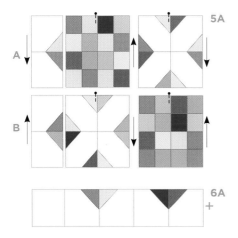

5 quilt center

Arrange the blocks into a 6 x 7 grid, alternating 16-patch blocks with X-blocks across in rows, and down in columns (rows **A** & **B**). **5A** Most seams will nest if blocks are kept right side up (pin on the top edge).

Add a pieced border block at the beginning and end of each row, its snowballed corners next to the quilt center. If necessary, re-press their center seams so they nest with the blocks they connect to.

Sew blocks together side-to-side in rows, pressing seams in even rows to the right; in odd rows to the left. Then sew rows together.

6 final borders

Select (6) pieced blocks and sew them together end-to-end in one long strip, all snowballed corners along the one edge. Add a solid 4½″ square at the beginning and end of the strip. **6A**

Make (2). Press seams in the best direction for nesting. Attach one border to the top, the other to the bottom of the quilt.

For the tutorial and everything
you need to make this quilt visit:
www.msqc.co/blockspring15

beach
picnic

quilt designed by JENNY DOAN

Beach picnics were a regular part of our lives when the kids were growing up. At least once a week we threw a quilt in the car with a basket of goodies and headed to the beach for what we intended to be a peaceful afternoon. We usually told ourselves it was just a picnic; no one was going to get in the water (well maybe just our toes).

We made the short drive and pulled off the road in a good spot, a cove with tide pools and a bit of sand that offered some privacy and shelter from the wind. We spread the quilt out on the sand with intentions just to eat lunch, but inevitably our plans slowly began to change. The inevitable building of sand castles began, but it takes a little bit of water to make the sand stick together and hold a shape, so one must venture to the water—just a little bit. It's hard not to get pants a bit wet as we waded out with a bucket to gather water. But then we got wetter still whenever we hunted shells

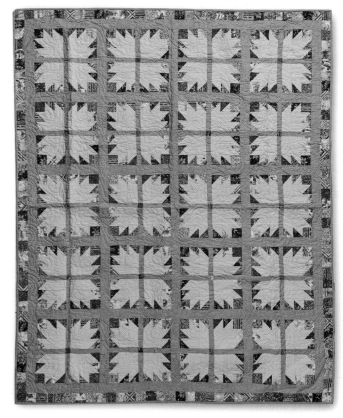

"Once we gave up the idea of a nice, quiet (dry) day in the sand, we laughed and played away all afternoon."

or chased down feathers and pieces of driftwood in the surf. Before we knew it, we were splashing and swimming and body surfing in the waves. Once we gave up the idea of a nice, quiet (dry) day in the sand, we laughed and played away all afternoon.

After a day at the beach, have you ever tried to get in your car without bringing any sand with you? Have you ever tried that with a passel of kids? It doesn't work with one person and you can bet your britches it doesn't work with nine! Still, at the end of the day I did what I could to minimize the amount of beach we brought home with us. It was quite a production getting kids to brush off, strip away wet clothes, and get in the car with as little mess as possible.

One time, in our haste to get in the car, we left our quilt on the beach. We went back for it, but it was already gone. I have wondered about the life it has lived since. Someone must have loved it enough to pick it up off the sand and take it home. I hope it provided comfort. I hope it never had to sit on a shelf in a closet. I hope it had a good life and saw many more beach picnics and plenty of sand.

materials

makes a 67" X 82" quilt

QUILT TOP
- (1) 2½" WOF roll print
- (1) 2½" WOF roll solid for bear paws
- 2 yds sashing solid

BINDING
- ¾ yd coordinating fabric

BACKING
- 5 yds 44" **OR** 2¼ yds 90" wide

SAMPLE QUILT
- **French Quarter**
  by Dover Hill for Benartex
- **Bella Solids Home Town Sky (177)** by
  Moda Fabrics
- **Weave Tan (18)** by Moda Fabrics

1 cut & select

Cut all WOF print strips into 2½"
squares.

From the solid WOF strips, cut:
- (5) into 2½" squares
- (18) into 4½" segments &
- (14) into 6½" segments

2 make a bear paw

*In this step, press all solid strips away
from the 2½" print square.*

The block is built along 2 adjacent
sides of a 2½" print square in a partial
log cabin. When adding solid segments, always cross the seam just
sewn.

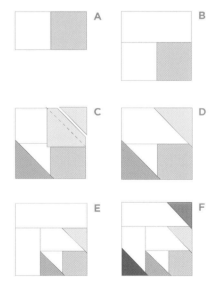

3A

3B

3C

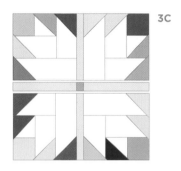

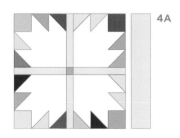

4A

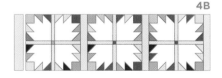

4B

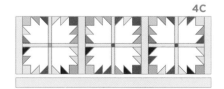

4C

A RST, sew a solid to a print square.

B Add a solid 4½" strip to the adjacent side of the print square.

C Use (2) print 2½" squares to snowball the solid corners on either side of the original print square. Trim away excess fabric.

D Press open.

E Add another 4½" segment to the block; and a 6½" segment to that.

F Again, snowball the solid corners, trim and press open.

Repeat for a total of (80) bear paws.

Block size: 6½" x 6½"

3 build the block

Always press to the sashing.

From the sashing fabric, cut:
    (14) 1½" WOF strips; subcut into (80) 6½" segments

Select (20) various 2½" *print* squares and trim to 1½." These are cornerstones.

Attach (2) 6½" sashing segments to opposite sides of a cornerstone making one long strip. Make 20 & set aside. **3A**

Sew (2) bear paws together with a 6½" sashing segment between them. The 2½" print corner squares should be positioned along the same edge but in opposing corners. **3B**

Select (2) of these bear paw pairs to make a full block. Sew a sashing + cornerstone unit between the pairs. **3C** Each corner of the final block will be a print square. Make (20) total.

Block size: 13½" x 13½"

4 quilt center

From the remaining sashing fabric, cut:
    (18) 2½" WOF strips; subcut (9) into (25) 13½" segments.

Sew a 13½" sashing segment to the right side of each block. **4A**

Lay the blocks into a 4 x 5 setting.

Sew blocks to each other side-to-side into rows. Add an additional 13½" sashing segment to the beginning of each row. **4B**

Sew the remaining (9) 2½" WOF sashing strips together end-to-end. Cut (6) 62½" horizontal sashing strips. Measure your rows to be sure!

Attach (5) strips to the bottom of each row horizontally. **4C**

Sew rows together. Attach the last sashing strip to the top.

Quilt Center size: 62½" x 77½"

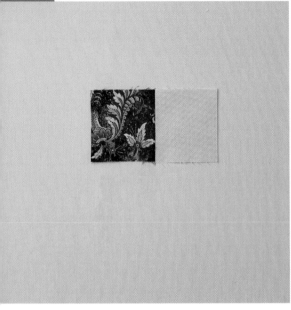

1 Start by sewing a print and solid square to each other. Step 2

2 Add a 4½″ strip to the adjacent side of the print square. Step 2

3 Snowball the solid corners closest to the print square. Then add solid strips again. Step 2

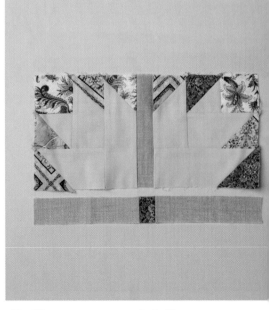

4 Continue snowballing corners and adding strips. Notice how the snowballed corners follow two sides of the original print square. Step 2

5 One complete bear paw is one quarter of a block. Step 2

6 2 bear paws are connected with a vertical sashing strip. Then a horizontal sashing strip with a cornerstone is added to the block. Step 3

A

C

D

B

5 pieced border

Sew (31) 2½″ print squares together in a long strip. Press all seams to the same side. Make (2) & cut at 62½.″ *Measure your quilt's actual width before cutting.* Attach one to the top; one to the bottom of the quilt. A & B

Repeat for the quilt sides with (41) print squares and cut to 81½.″ *Again, measure your quilt's length.* Make (2) & attach to each side. C & D

6 quilt & bind

Layer quilt top on batting and backing and quilt the way you like. Square up all raw edges.

Cut (8) 2½″ strips from binding fabric to finish. See *construction basics* for greater detail.

For the tutorial and everything
you need to make this quilt visit:
www.msqc.co/blockspring15

orange
peel

designed by JENNY DOAN

I've always loved collecting seashells. At first glance, they seem so tiny and uniform, but each one is actually packed with incredible detail, beauty, and originality.

Growing up, my favorite beach was dotted with pale violet, olive-shaped shells called purple dwarves. When purple dwarves get worn down by sand and waves, they develop a little hole at one end which makes them perfect for stringing on bracelets. I practically had enough shell bracelets to start a boutique.

Because those shells were so common at my special beach, I thought that all the ocean was brimming with purple dwarves. It wasn't until later in life that I visited enough other beaches to realize that every beach has a different variety of shells. Most of the beaches of the world have their own lovely shells and don't have a single purple dwarf.

All these years later, I have just one of my old shell bracelets left, and it is special to me because now I know how unique it is, both the bracelet itself and the individual shells that comprise it. Despite being of the same variety, the shells come in a number of hues and designs. Some are a different shade of purple, some with a hint of red, some with a sharper tip. No two curve in the same swirl.

“ Most of the beaches of the world have their own lovely shells and don't have a single purple dwarf. „

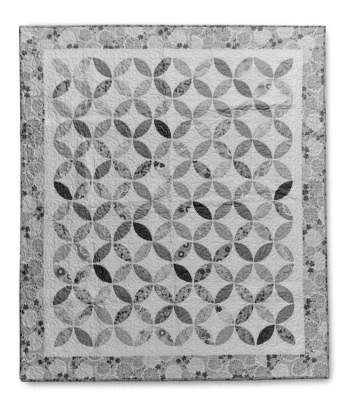

Of course, we are all like that in some way, aren't we? The more people I meet the more I know that to be true. The details that make us different also make us beautiful. Maybe that's one of the reasons I love quilting: the details, the variety, and the way no two can ever be the same no matter how hard you may try. There's an awful lot of beauty in this world. Just call me a collector.

materials

makes a 68" X 77" quilt

QUILT TOP
- (4) 5" square packs print
- (4) 5" square packs solid
- ½ yd inner border solid
  (same color as solid square packs)
- 1 yd outer border

BINDING
- ¾ yd coordinating fabric

BACKING
- 4¼ yds 44" **OR** 2¼ yds 90" wide

ADD'L MATERIALS
- MSQC Small Football Ruler
- 5¼ yds Pellon Featherweight to Midweight fusible interfacing *(911FFPWHT)*

SAMPLE QUILT
- **True Luck** by Stephanie Ryan for Moda Fabrics
- **Bella Solids White (98)** by Moda Fabrics

1 cut & select

Using the *MSQC Small Football Ruler*, cut the petal shape from all 5" print squares.

Cut the same number of petal shapes from fusible interfacing *(5 slanted petals per 5½" x 20")*. It may be easiest to trace the ruler and use scissors to cut the shapes out. Mark the dots of the ruler with a pencil on the non-glue side of the interfacing. **1A**

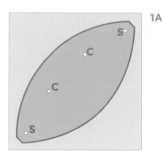

1A

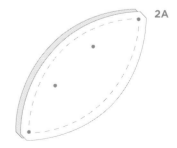

2A

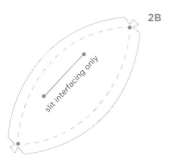

2B

2C

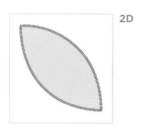

2D

2 appliqué

Pair a fabric petal with an interfacing petal, glue side to the fabric's right side, marked dots visible.

With the interfacing side up, sew a ¼" around the perimeter pivoting at the (2) S dots. 2A

To turn the petal right side out, slice the interfacing layer open between the (2) C dots located within the petal. Clip the seam allowances and turn. Push out the petal. 2B

Position the petal at a 45° angle across a 5" solid square, interfacing toward the square. Fuse the petal.

Repeat, fusing each petal to a 5" solid square. 2C

Machine stitch the petal to the background with either a straight, zig-zag, or blanket stitch. 2D

3 quilt center

Arrange the petal blocks in an eye-pleasing 12 x 14 setting. Alternate the angle of each petal across in rows and down in columns. Use an A B A B sequence for odd rows; a B A B A sequence for even rows. 3A

Once you are pleased with the layout begin sewing blocks together in rows side-to-side. Press seams in odd rows to

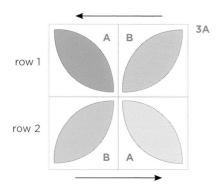

3A

row 1

row 2

A   B

B   A

one side; in even rows to the opposite side.

Sew rows together, nesting seams as you go. Press.

Quilt Center Size: 54½" x 63½"

4 borders

From the inner border fabric cut (7) 2½" WOF strips. Follow steps in *construction basics* to attach to the quilt. A-D Press to the borders.

Cut (7) 5" WOF strips of outer border fabric. Attach to the quilt in the same manner as the inner border.

5 quilt & bind

Layer quilt top on batting and backing and quilt the way you like. Square up all raw edges.

Cut (8) 2½" WOF strips from binding fabric to finish. See *construction basics* for greater detail.

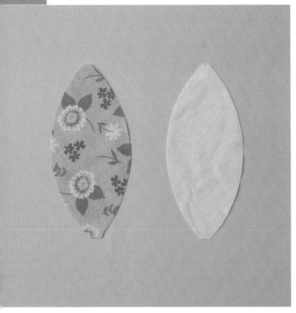

1 Cut the same number of petal interfacings as you have print petals. Step 1

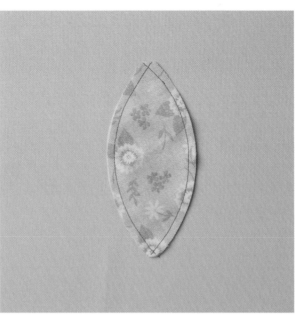

2 Pair a petal with the interfacing petal, glue side against the fabric petal's print side. Sew the two together around the entire perimeter. Step 2

3 Slice through the interfacing only. Pull it away from the fabric petal to cut.

4 Turn the petal right side out through the opening and push out the shape. Step 2

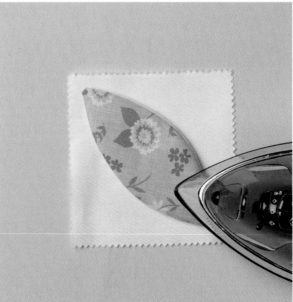

5 Center the petal on a solid square at a 45 degree angle. Fuse into place. Step 2

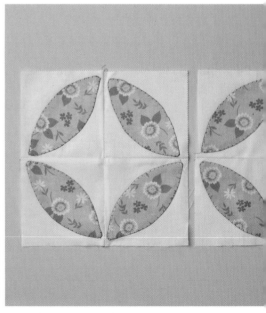

6 Alternate the petal's angle across in rows and down in columns as you lay out the blocks. Step 3

A

C  D

B

sandy
sunrise

designed by JENNY DOAN

When I was a teenager, I got it into my head that I wanted to go to the beach to watch the sunrise. It seemed like such an inspiring adventure, one for which I was even willing to sacrifice a little sleep. I asked my mom for permission and, perhaps with a knowing smile, she consented.

The next day I woke up very early and drove through the quiet darkness to the beach. With a quilt wrapped around my shoulders, I walked along the sand and nestled myself in the dunes with my eyes fixed on the horizon. As I sat and waited, it got lighter and lighter— and my back got warmer and warmer. Finally, with a flash of realization, I turned around to discover that the sun had come up behind me! Somehow, even though I

had been a California girl all my life, it never occurred to me that, on the west coast, the sun does not rise over the ocean even if an eager, young teenager wakes up extra early to watch.

When I got home I asked Mom why she had let me go when she obviously knew what would happen. "Some lessons are best learned in person," Mom explained.

I have since traveled many times to the east coast of the United States to watch the sunrise over the ocean, and it never ceases to fill my heart with serene excitement. There is something special about sunrise and sunset. Sometimes when I am driving along the road by the ocean as the sun is about to rise or set, I notice all the cars pulling over and everyone getting out to watch. No one speaks and there is such a feeling of reverence and awe at this magical

scene. It is as if time stands still while everything is quiet if just for a moment. Strangely, I can never decide whether this makes me feel very tiny or larger than life.

Whether it is a delicate sunrise over the Atlantic ocean, or a blazing sunset over the Pacific, it is a wonderful thing to witness that instant when the sun finally touches the horizon.

materials

makes a 50" X 50" quilt

QUILT TOP
- (3) 5" square packs print
- (1) 5" square pack solid
- ½ yd solid/inner border fabric

BINDING
- ½ yd coordinating fabric

BACKING
- 3¼ yds coordinating fabric

SAMPLE QUILT
- **Ophelia** by Nancy Gere for Windham
- **Bella Solids Natural (11)** by Moda Fabrics

1 cut & select

Iron a diagonal fold into (32) of the solid 5" squares. This will be the sewing line. Pair these RST with (32) random 5" print squares.

Stitch on the fold. **1A** Chain piece the pairs one after another. Clip apart. Trim excess fabric ¼" from the stitching. **1B** Press open.

Yield: (32) HST **1C**

2 build the block

Select (2) 5" squares and (2) HSTs randomly to build 2 different rows: **A & B. 2A**

Make (8) **A** rows & (8) **B** rows.

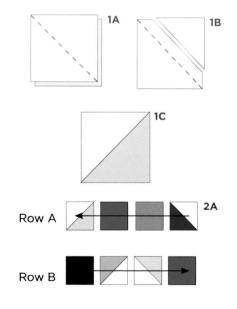

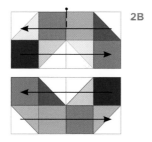

2B

Before sewing the blocks together, re-press any HST seams so that they are facing in the direction of the pressing arrows.

Sew the blocks in rows together side-to-side and press the seams following the arrows as well.

Sew a row **A** to the top of a row **B**, nesting seams at each intersection. Do not press horizontal seams yet. This **AB** unit is a half-block.

Turn an **AB** unit upside down and sew it to another **AB** unit. Mark the top of the block with a pin. The seams of its top row should be pressed to the left. **2B** Make (4).

Block size: 18½" x 18½"

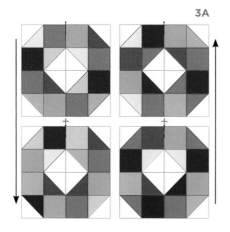

3A

3 arrange

The (4) blocks are arranged in a 2 x 2 setting. Orient the top of the block either right side up, or upside down, but not sideways. **3A**

Now press the horizontal seams of the blocks in the first column (odd), down; the horizontal seams of the second column (even), up.

Sew blocks together in columns first; then sew the columns to each other. The seams should nest easily. Press vertical seam(s) between columns open.

Quilt Center Size: 36½" x 36½"

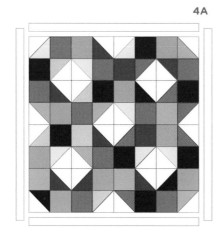

4A

4 inner border

From the inner border fabric cut (4) 2½" strips. Follow steps in *construction basics* to attach to the quilt. Press to the borders. **4A**

5 pieced border

For custom borders, follow border instructions in the *construction basics* section (page 6).

Sew (9) 5" print squares together for each top & bottom border. Trim to 40½"—measure your quilt top before cutting. Attach to the quilt.

Press to the inner border.

Next, sew (11) 5" print squares together for each side border. Trim to 49½"—again, measure your own quilt top. Attach to either side.

Press to the inner border. **5A**

6 quilt & bind

Layer quilt top on batting and backing and quilt the way you like. Square up all raw edges.

Cut (6) 2½" strips from binding fabric to finish. See *construction basics* for greater detail.

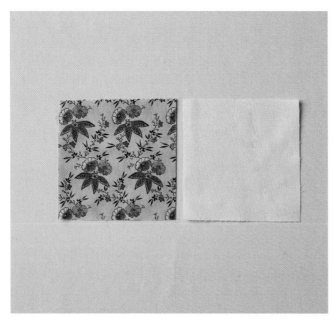

1 Use a print and a solid 5″ square to make the half square triangles (HSTs) needed in the block. Step 1

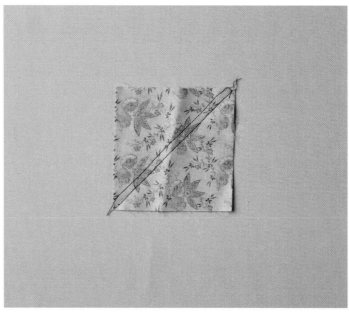

2 Sew across the pair diagonally from corner to corner. If you want, you can sew another line of stitching ½″ to one side to make another HST for another project. Step 1

3 Arrange 4 HSTs and 4 print squares into a row A and a row B. Then sew a row A to the top of a Row B. This is half a block—an AB unit. Step 2

4 Flip one AB unit upside down and sew it to another AB unit: one circle block. Step 2

Cuddle Tips & Tricks

We love the look and feel of Cuddle. It's such a versatile fabric. The quilts we have made with Cuddle have very quickly become the best loved quilts in our homes. Here's a great list of tips and tricks to help you start using this fabulous fabric! Give it a try! You'll be glad you did!

Cutting

- You will get "cuddle dust" when you cut Cuddle; the longer the fibers, the more "dust." To control this, cut shorter Cuddle fabrics with a rotary cutter, remove from cutting surface, and place in dryer with damp wash cloth on low heat for about 10 minutes.

- For longer fiber Cuddle such as rose Cuddle, shag, frizzy and furs: draw cutting line on backside of fabric, and with scissors, cut through the backing only. Then pull apart and place in dryer.

- Keep a vacuum cleaner nearby and vacuum along cutting lines before moving cut fabric. Be extra careful with cut fabric so you don't suck it up. We like to use a small shop vac here in the studio.

- When cutting, check nap BEFORE you cut each piece to be sure it is going in the right direction.

- Cuddle does not fray. For a great edge finish on double sided Cuddle and bindings, you may use a rotary cutter with a pinking or wave blade.

- When using pattern pieces, do not pin through layers. Pre-cut your pattern pieces and hold in place with pattern weights or rulers (Empty coffee cups and tuna or soup cans work great). Tissue paper patterns can be ironed to the waxy side of freezer paper and cut out; use pattern weights to hold in place. If cutting multiple size patterns, trace desired size

onto freezer paper, paper side up, cut out pattern pieces, add pattern weights, and cut out with rotary cutter. The freezer paper is a good guideline because it sits on top of the fabric and provides a more precise cut.

Sewing

- Be aware of straight of grain and stretch. When using strips, cut to size and pin in place to keep fabric from stretching or shrinking.

- Take your time when sewing with Cuddle fabrics. A little patience goes a long way!

- Use pins. With this material you need to use pins. It slides under the needle, so for straight seams and limited heartache, pin it a lot! When pinning fabrics together use sturdy flower head pins. They show up easily in the cuddle nap and if you should accidentally leave a pin in the seam, the metal shaft can be removed with pliers and the top can stay inside the project and not cause any injuries.

- If you plan on doing a lot of sewing with Cuddle fabric, a walking foot is worth the investment. A walking foot is a special foot apparatus that makes it so the cloth has feed dogs feeding it on the top as well as beneath. It makes it so the fabric can't slide under the needle, and helps keep stitches even. It also allows you to sew through thick sections of fabric with little difficulty. It basically gives your machine super powers! It's a good tool for a sewist

to have in her toolkit. The downside to a walking foot is that it can't handle turns, so you either have to sew a few stitches and manually turn the fabric yourself at gradual increments, or forgo the walking foot altogether for a curvy piece.

- Try not to pull fabrics through, let your walking foot and feed dogs do the work.

- Use a size 90/14 ballpoint (stretch) needle for piecing.

- Lengthen the stitch length to 3-3.5 mm. This will give the fibers room to nest together and not distort your seams.

- Use a ⅜ to ½ inch seam allowance consistently throughout your project. Your walking foot can act as a guide. Change needle position if needed.

- Use a pressing sheet between fabric and iron. Press lightly and be very careful with embossed and dimpled fabrics.

- For "sandwiching" and appliqué, spray adhesives work for holding batting, backing, and fabrics together. Be sure to ventilate area when spraying. 505 Spray and Fix from Odif is a good product. Use freezer paper, paper side up, to protect projects from overspray. You can also use a glue stick to hold smaller pieces in place.

- The blind hem stitch lengthened to 3mm and 5mm wide is a good one to use for

appliqué. The stitch will be hidden in the fibers. Straight stitch, blanket, and zig-zag are also good options. Be sure to test stitches and lengthen as needed.

Binding

- Cut binding strips 2 inches X width of fabric (you could cut the strips using a pinking blade if desired).
- Lay out strips so nap is going the same direction.
- Join strips, right sides together using plus sign method.
- Your binding will be a single layer. Stitch binding to the front of quilt using traditional methods for joining ends and turning corners.
- Flip quilt over, fold the binding to fit tight against the stitching line edge.
- Topstitch raw edge using a zig zag, serpentine, or other decorative stitch.

Care

- Machine wash, gentle cycle, cold water.
- Machine dry, low heat. Some embossed and longer fibers may change appearance slightly after drying. It will surprise you how fast the finished projects dry, so check after 20 minutes. Projects without batting will dry very quickly.

I love seeking out new ways to express my creativity. I always have a project or two running through my mind. When my family asked if I wanted to come and design the window displays I was thrilled! I live about four hours from them and this was the perfect way for me to come and play in the fabric and sewing fun while completely indulging my creative tendencies!

Finding inspiration for the windows is very natural for me. I get ideas from everything I see. These ideas may come from family events, pictures, color trends, or maybe even a birthday card. I'll see an element that strikes me as beautiful or interesting and the ideas begin to grow in my head. Often I'll base the window designs on things I find online, in books or magazines. I love what I do!

Hillary Sperry
MSQC Window Design Artist

LICENSED TO
SEW

✣ MISSOURI STAR QUILT CO. ✣

Our very talented sister Hillary has been working hard to decorate our shop windows and we think she's done a fabulous job. These photos are from the windows for our newest shop Licensed to Sew. She's made an adorable scene of quilted rolling hills and fluffy white clouds, with the cutest crocheted Super heroes flying around above the town. If you're in Hamilton, be sure to stop and take a look at this window display.

Our Licensed to Sew shop will feature all of our licensed and novelty style fabrics. Some of them include but are not limited to Disney(Frozen), Sports, NFL, MLB, NBA, College Teams, Food, Sewing, Comic Book (Superman, Batman, Wonder Woman), Extreme Sports, Star Trek, Angry Birds, Farm life, Motorcycles, Fish, etc. If you have a hobby or just something you love, we will probably have a fabric for you! As an added bonus it connects to Penney's quilt shop, the home of our solids and basic lines. Be sure to check out the gorgeous windows in all of our shops.

beach picnic

QUILT SIZE
67" X 82"

DESIGNED BY
Jenny Doan

PIECED BY
Jenny Doan

QUILTED BY
Marsha Rannabargar

QUILT TOP
(1) 2½" WOF roll print
(1) 2½" WOF roll solid for bear paws
2 yds sashing solid

BINDING
¾ yd coordinating fabric

BACKING
5 yds 44" **OR** 2¼ yds 90" wide

SAMPLE QUILT
French Quarter
by Dover Hill for Benartex
**Bella Solids Home Town Sky
(177)** by Moda Fabrics
Weave Tan (18) by Moda Fabrics

ONLINE TUTORIALS
msqc.co/blockspring15

QUILTING
Variety

QUILT PATTERN
pg 62

crazy birds

QUILT SIZE
61½" X 71"

DESIGNED BY
Jenny Doan

PIECED BY
Jenny Doan

QUILTED BY
Sandi Gaunce

QUILT TOP
(1) 2½" WOF roll print
(1) 10" square pack solid **OR** 1¼ yds
   background solid fabric
1¼ yds for crazy birds
½ yd inner border solid (same as solid)
1 yd outer border

BINDING
½ yd coordinating fabric

BACKING
4 yds coordinating fabric

ADD'L MATERIALS
2¼ yds 18" wide Heat 'n Bond

SAMPLE QUILT
Gardenvale by Jen Kingswell for
Moda Fabrics
Kona Cotton Ash (1007) by Robert
Kaufman
Pink Grunge by Moda Fabrics

ONLINE TUTORIALS
msqc.co/blockspring15

QUILTING
Birds

PATTERN
pg 24

dressed
to the nines

QUILT SIZE
68" X 94"

DESIGNED BY
Jenny Doan

PIECED BY
Cindy Morris

QUILTED BY
Kaitlyn Adams

QUILT TOP
(5) 5" square packs print
½ yd accent fabric
½ yd inner border
1½ yds outer border

BINDING
¾ yd coordinating fabric

BACKING
5¾ yds 44" **OR** 3 yds 90" wide

SAMPLE QUILT
Princess Life by Robert Kaufman

ONLINE TUTORIAL
msqc.co/blockspring15

QUILTING
Cotton Candy

PATTERN
pg 40

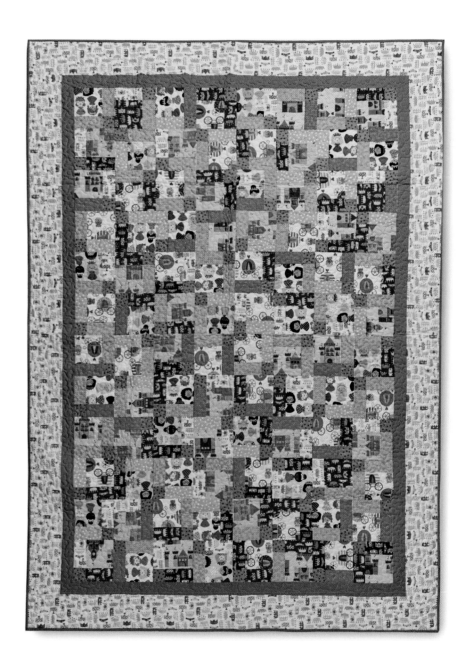

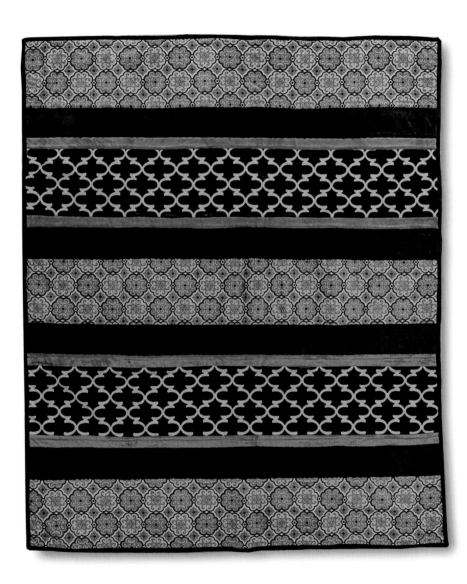

firenze

QUILT SIZE
60" X 68"

DESIGNED BY
Shannon Fabrics

PIECED BY
Shannon Fabrics

QUILT TOP
All fabrics 60" wide
1 yd Green Tile
⅔ yd Navy Tile
1 yd Navy Solid
⅓ yd Teal Solid

BACKING
2 yd coordinating fabric

ADDITIONAL MATERIALS
505 Quilt Basting Spray
Batting 60" x 78"

SAMPLE QUILT
Bella Vita by Shannon Fabrics

ONLINE TUTORIALS
msqc.co/blockspring15

QUILT PATTERN
pg 48

goodnight, irene

QUILT SIZE
57" X 65"

DESIGNED BY
Jenny Doan

PIECED BY
Jenny Doan

QUILTED BY
Sandi Gaunce

QUILT TOP
(4) 5" square packs print
(3) 5" square packs solid + ¼ yd
   OR 2¼ yds solid

BINDING
½ yd coordinating fabric

BACKING
3¾ yds coordinating fabric

SAMPLE QUILT
Floribella by Emily Taylor for
Riley Blake
**Cotton Supreme Optical White
(59)** by RJR

ONLINE TUTORIALS
msqc.co/blockspring15

QUILTING
Simply Swirly

QUILT PATTERN
PG 54

orange peel

QUILT SIZE
68" X 77"

DESIGNED BY
Jenny Doan

PIECED BY
Carol Henderson

QUILTED BY
Daniela Kirk

QUILT TOP
(4) 5" square packs print
(4) 5" square packs solid
½ yd inner border solid *(same color as solid square packs)*
1 yd outer border

BINDING
¾ yd coordinating fabric

BACKING
4¼ yds 44" **OR** 2¼ yds 90" wide

ADD'L MATERIALS
MSQC Small Football Ruler
 (optional)
5¼ yds Pellon Featherweight
 to Midweight fusible
 interfacing *(911FFPWHT)*

SAMPLE QUILT
True Luck by Stephanie Ryan for Moda Fabrics
Bella Solids White (98) by Moda Fabrics

ONLINE TUTORIALS
msqc.co/blockspring15

QUILTING
Simply Swirly

PATTERN
PG 70

pennant flags

QUILT SIZE
64¼" X 84"

DESIGNED BY
Jenny Doan

PIECED BY
Jenny Doan

QUILTED BY
Tia Gilliam

QUILT TOP
(1) 10" square pack print
   (enough for 2 quilts)
3¼ yds background solid
1 yd outer border

BINDING
¾ yd coordinating fabric

BACKING
5 yds **OR** 2 yds 90" wide

ADDITIONAL MATERIALS
MSQC Large Simple Wedge
9½ yds ¾" Rickrack

SAMPLE QUILT
Daysail by Bonnie & Camille for
Moda Fabrics
Bella Solids White (98) by
Moda Fabrics

ONLINE TUTORIALS
msqc.co/blockspring15

QUILTING
Free Swirls

QUILT PATTERN
PG 32

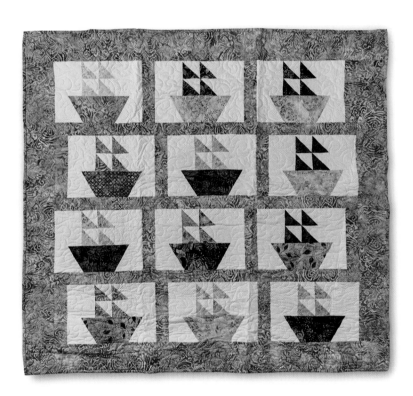

sail
away

QUILT SIZE
50½" X 53"

DESIGNED BY
Jenny Doan

PIECED BY
Kelly McKenzie

QUILTED BY
Amy Gertz

QUILT TOP
 (1) 10" square pack print **OR**
        (12) 10" various print squares
1½ yds background solid

SASHING/BORDER/BINDING
1¾ yds coordinating fabric

BACKING
3¼ yds coordinating fabric

ADD'L MATERIALS
MSQC 10" Half Hexagon Ruler

SAMPLE QUILT
Artisan Batiks Splendid 3 by Lunn
Studios for Robert Kaufman
Kona Cotton White (1387) by
Robert Kaufman

ONLINE TUTORIALS
msqc.co/blockspring15

QUILTING
Free Swirls

QUILT PATTERN
PG 8

sandy
sunrise

QUILT SIZE
50" X 50"

DESIGNED BY
Jenny Doan

PIECED BY
Kelly McKenzie

QUILTED BY
Daniela Kirk

QUILT TOP
(3) 5" square packs print
(1) 5" square pack solid
½ yd solid/inner border fabric

BINDING
½ yd coordinating fabric

BACKING
3¼ yds coordinating fabric

SAMPLE QUILT
Ophelia by Nancy Gere for
Windham
Bella Solids Natural (11) by Moda
Fabrics

ONLINE TUTORIALS
msqc.co/blockspring15

QUILT PATTERN
PG 78

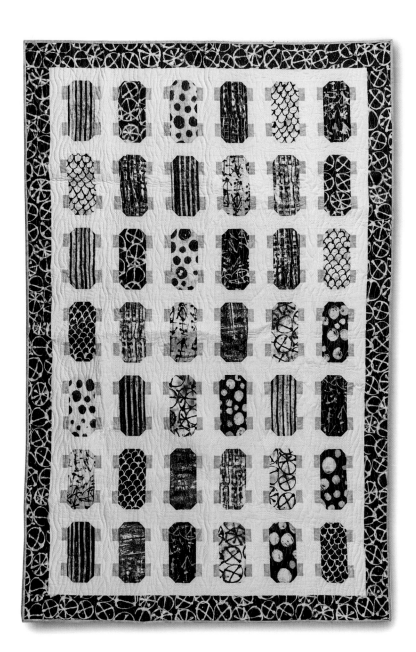

skateboards

QUILT SIZE
61" X 90½"

DESIGNED BY
Jenny Doan

PIECED BY
Kelly McKenzie

QUILTED BY
Mari Zullig

QUILT TOP
(1) 10" square pack print
   (enough for 2 quilts)
2¾ yds background solid
½ yd green for wheels
1 yd outer border

BINDING
¾ yd coordinating fabric

BACKING
3½ yds 44" or 2¼ yds 90" wide

SAMPLE QUILT
Back & White by Marcia Derse for Windham
Bella Solids White (98) by Moda Fabrics
Handspray Jewel Box Lime Green (001) by RJR

ONLINE TUTORIALS
msqc.co/blockspring15

QUILTING
Flame

QUILT PATTERN
pg 16

general guidelines

- All seams are ¼" inch unless directions specify differently.

- Cutting instructions are given at the point when cutting is required.

- Precuts are not prewashed; therefore do not prewash other fabrics in the project

- All strips are cut WOF

- Remove all selvages

- All yardages based on 42" WOF

ACRONYMS USED

MSQC Missouri Star Quilt Co.

RST right sides together

WST wrong sides together

HST half square triangle

WOF width of fabric

LOF length of fabric

pre-cut glossary

5" SQUARES

1 = (42) 5" squares or ¾ yd of fabric

1 = baby

2 = crib

3 = lap

4 = twin

2½" STRIPS

1 = (40) 2½" strips cut the width of fabric
       or 2¾ yds of fabric

1 = a twin

2 = queen

10" SQUARES

1 = (42) 10" squares of fabric: 2¾ yds total

1 = a twin

2 = queen

When we mention a precut, we are basing the pattern on a 40-42 count pack. Not all precuts have the same count, so be sure to check the count on your precut to make sure you have enough pieces to complete your project.

press seams

- Use a steam iron on the cotton setting.

- Iron the seam just as it was sewn RST. This "sets" the seam.

- With dark fabric on top, lift the dark fabric and press back.

- The seam allowance is pressed to the dark side. Some patterns may direct otherwise for certain situations.

- Follow pressing arrows in the diagrams when indicated.

- Press toward borders. Pieced borders may demand otherwise.

- Press diagonal seams open on binding to reduce bulk.

borders

- Always measure the quilt top 3 times before cutting borders.
- Start with the width and measure the top edge, middle and bottom.
- Folding the quilt in half is a quick way to find the middle.
- Take the average of those 3 measurements.
- Cut 2 border strips to that size. Piece strips together if needed.

- Attach 1 to the top, 1 to the bottom.
- Position the border fabric on top as you sew. The feed dogs can act like rufflers. Having the border on top will prevent waviness and keep the quilt straight.
- Repeat this process for the side borders, measuring the length 3 times.
- Include the newly attached top and bottom borders in your measurements.
- Press to the borders.

binding

find a video tutorial at: www.msqc.co/006

- Use 2½" strips for binding.
- Sew strips end-to-end into one long strip with diagonal seams, aka plus sign method (next). Press seams open.
- Fold in half lengthwise WST and press.
- The entire length should equal the outside dimension of the quilt plus 15" - 20."

plus sign method

- Lay one strip across the other as if to make a plus sign RST.
- Sew from top inside to bottom outside corners crossing the intersections of fabric as you sew. Trim excess to ¼" seam allowance.
- Press seam open.

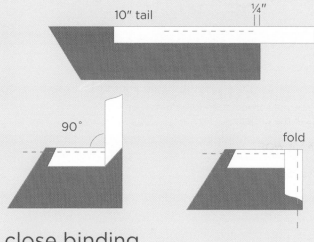

attach binding

- Match raw edges of folded binding to the quilt top edge.
- Leave a 10" tail at the beginning.
- Use a ¼" seam allowance.
- Start in the middle of a long straight side.

find a video tutorial at: www.msqc.co/001

miter corners

- Stop sewing ¼" before the corner.
- Move the quilt out from under the pressure foot.
- Clip the threads.
- Flip the binding up at a 90° angle to the edge just sewn.
- Fold the binding down along the next side to be sewn aligning raw edges.
- The fold will lie along the edge just completed.
- Begin sewing on the fold.

close binding

MSQC recommends The Binding Tool from TQM Products to finish binding perfectly every time.

- Stop sewing when you have 12" left to reach the start.
- Where the binding tails come together trim excess leaving only 2½" of overlap.
- It helps to pin or clip the quilt together at the two points where the binding starts and stops. This takes the pressure off of the binding tails while you work.
- Use the plus sign method to sew the two binding ends together, except this time when making the plus sign, match the edges. Using a pencil, mark your sewing line since you won't be able to see where the corners intersect. Sew across.

plus sign with matched edges

- Trim off excess; press seam open.
- Fold in half WST and align all raw edges to the quilt top.
- Sew this last binding section to the quilt. Press.
- Turn the folded edge of the binding around to the back of the quilt and tack into place with an invisible stitch or machine stitch if you wish.

HIDEAWAY IN QUILT TOWN, USA

PART 1
Quilting Retreat

——— A JENNY DOAN MYSTERY ———

written by Steve Westover

Amber Kim scrubbed pink smoothie from the floor beneath her desk, cursing her usual clumsiness. The keyboard and the phone escaped unscathed, this time, but her charcoal pinstripe slacks and the beige carpet hadn't been so fortunate. Taking a short break from the scrubbing, Amber knelt tall to stretch as she peered through the plate glass door dividing her office from the remainder of the law firm. Except for John Thurman, the firm's managing partner, Amber was alone and thankful for the anonymity of her late evening mishap. She adjusted her earbuds and turned on her favorite Pandora station. Her black ponytail swayed in rhythm with the music, slowly at first but then with vigor as the chorus blasted in her ears. Exasperated to be cleaning instead of working on her brief Amber cranked the volume and scrubbed.

By the end of the third song only a rosy hint of smoothie remained and Amber knew the rest would only be cured by professionals. Standing, she straightened her blouse and rubbed her knees before slumping into her high-back leather chair. She dabbed the perspiration on her forehead as she prepared to dive back into her writing when from across the lobby movement drew her attention to Thurman's office. The glass door was closed and he stood, fidgeting behind his desk while two men stood in front of him. Startled, Amber realized she and John weren't alone after all. She hadn't noticed anyone come in but that was probably the fault of the music and her smoothie fiasco.

Amber tossed her earbuds onto the desk and adjusted her glasses higher on her nose as she studied the men who looked identical from a distance. They stood the same height, their hair

was cropped military style and their well-tailored suits wrapped them gorgeously in a package of wealth. Amber squinted at the backs of the men trying to recognize them when the unmistakable blast of a handgun shattered the silence.

Amber's eyes widened with horror as John Thurman clutched his chest. She gasped and then as one of the men turned in place, she dropped onto the pink tinged floor beneath her desk. The chair began to roll but she steadied it with her hand, forcing it into stillness. She knelt on all fours, panting from the shock as John's lifeless body flopped to the floor. Panic filled her mind. Amber gulped once and then attempted to steady her nerves as she peeked around the corner of her desk.

Both men remained in Thurman's office but they faced hers, staring. Amber's panic turned to terror. She grabbed the back of her neck as thoughts swirled through her mind. *Why didn't they make sure they were alone before killing John? Wait, maybe John's not dead. Maybe...* Amber struggled to control her thoughts but wondered why the men hadn't noticed her before as hers was the only other light in the entire firm. Then she remembered the smoothie on the carpet and how she must have been hidden from view.

Amber cautiously peaked around the corner of the desk. The two fine-suited men strode down the long hallway in her direction. Amber forced herself to breath as she looked past the killers to John Thurman whose body was mostly hidden behind his desk. She could see one open hand, John's hand, lying on the floor, motionless.

Maybe they'll just glance inside and then leave, she thought hopefully. "No, don't be stupid," she scolded herself quietly. *The lights, the computer.* They'll find me. She considered reaching atop her desk to turn off the computer but didn't dare reveal herself. Instead, she reached beneath her desk and unplugged the monitor. The men's steps grew louder and Amber's heart pounded in cadence.

Amber glanced around her office hoping for a hiding place to reveal itself but the only option was her restroom. It beckoned her but she resisted, knowing the armed men would spot her.

The steps grew louder and Amber could hear the men whispering but couldn't make out the words. With no time to debate the soundness of her hiding options Amber pulled her phone from a pocket and dialed the law firm's reception desk. Amber waited and then as the ring reverberated off the glass-walled firm, and the men turned, she raced on her hands and knees to her restroom. She propped it open just enough to slide in to the darkness and then stared through a crack hoping the phone had distracted the men. When the phone stopped ringing the men turned around and continued forward.

Amber gulped as the men entered the office. She stood in the small restroom with her back against the wall. She closed her eyes and listened as the men walked around her desk. They paused momentarily and then stepped toward the restroom door. Amber held her breath for complete silence. One man flipped the light switch and pushed the door inward as he stood at the threshold. The door rested against Amber's nose.

"Nobody's here," the man called out.

The other man paused but then replied. "Let's go."

As the man stepped away from the restroom Amber controlled a silent gasp for air. Footsteps padded down the hallway and a tear rolled down Amber's cheek. Amber crawled back to her desk. She watched and waited momentarily and then as the men entered John Thurman's office and crouched beside the body, she removed her heals and scurried out of the office, out of the firm and down a corridor.

Not daring to summon the elevator with its usual "ding" Amber raced to the stairwell, opening and closing the door with great care to ensure continued silence. She hurried down the stairs in bare feet, one hand gripping the railing while the other held her black pumps. Downstairs the expansive lobby offered no security. She quickly stepped into her shoes, swiped her access card to exit the building and then walked into the cool spring night. From the sidewalk Amber stared up at the building. The fourth floor light in John's office glowed and a shadowy figure stood in the window looking down at her. She gasped when she caught his gaze and then sprinted, in heels, the one block towards descending steps into the subway.

Amber climbed on the first available train, not caring where it would take her; the farther the better. She pulled out her phone but before she could dial 911 it rang. She stared at the display and quickly rejected the call. Seconds later the phone rang again. She clutched it as she stared at the display. She didn't answer. It rang again. She finally gave in.

"Amber Kim," a voice said calmly. Amber didn't respond but she heard a sinister chuckle on the other end of the call. "We know it's you."

"What do you want?" Amber asked, her voice taking on the rasp of an angry whisper.

"I'm glad you asked," the man said with a joviality that felt foreign and offensive. "All I need is you." Amber didn't respond. "Let's be honest here. You've seen something you shouldn't have. I'm sorry about that. Truly. It puts me in peril and I don't like being in peril. Do you understand?" Amber remained silent. "Look, there's nothing worse than uncertainty; that glance over your shoulder wondering when I'll find you," he said. "I will find you. It's a certainty. I find comfort in that even if you don't."

"What do you want from me?" Amber asked.

The man sighed loudly into the phone. "There's really only one thing. You must die." He paused. "I regret the necessity... but...you don't have to suffer. I'm a compassionate man."

"You expect me to let you kill me?" Amber scoffed with a nervous laugh.

The man's jovial tone hardened. "It's a certainty. I will find you and you won't like it when I do. Come to me and I'll be merciful. You won't feel a thing. I promise."

Amber yanked the phone from her ear as if it had just stung her. She stared and then hung up. Her shoulders rose with deep breaths while she contemplated the call. *They know who I am. How?* She grimaced at her foolish question. Not only could they deduce her involvement based on the light in her office but she had also used her access card to exit the building. Using the card was like a signature. *Not smart. And the phone. Can they track it?*

Amber stared at the phone hoping it would answer her question. The swirling panic and confusion of the night's events slowly gave way to the focus, logic, and decisiveness she was accustomed to. In an instant she knew what had to be done.

Amber didn't know who the men were or why the killed John, but she knew tracking the phone was a real possibility. At the next stop, she stepped off the train and tossed her phone and security card into a trash receptacle. She glanced at the debit card in her hand and knew that using it could lead them to her. But she needed money. She couldn't go home and she couldn't endanger a friend by asking for help. Racing up the subway steps to street level, Amber found an ATM and withdrew the daily maximum. It wouldn't get her far, but it was a start. Then rushing back into the subway she broke the card into pieces while waiting for the train that would take her to the 600 block of Harrison.

At the Greyhound Bus Lines depot Amber purchased, with cash, a one-way ticket on the next bus. Sitting in the darkness and anonymity of the Greyhound she pushed away the gruesome image of murder and allowed her mind to consider options and contingencies. After many quiet hours she drifted into a restless sleep.

After arriving at the Kansas City terminal Amber rubbed the weariness from her eyes as she considered her next move, knowing that the more she moved the safer she'd be. With no buses leaving Kansas City for hours she found a hotel room for the remainder of the night and slept with surprising soundness.

When she awoke, the murder of John Thurman felt like a distant dream but the eerily cheerful voice of the killer remained crisp in her mind. "You must die."

The words replayed over in her mind as she forced herself to eat the continental breakfast provided by the hotel. Despite the fog in her mind Amber felt the room energize as a cadre of women entered. They ate and talked excitedly about their pending adventure. Amber paid scant attention, focusing instead on her problems.

"Dear, are you a quilter?" Amber heard a soft voice ask the question but didn't register that it was directed to her. "Dear, are you all right?"

Amber widened her eyes and sat up straight as her interest shifted from her bagel to the silver-haired woman addressing her. She smiled. "Yes, I'm fine. Thank you." She met the gaze of the older women. "Oh... and no. I don't quilt."

"Pity," another woman muttered in a craggily, three-hundred year old voice.

Amber forced a grin. "I'm sure it's great."

"Oh it is. We're on a pilgrimage to visit the quilting mecca. We've been planning for months."

"I hope you have a wonderful day," Amber said as her voice caught on the emotion of knowing that her day, and every day thereafter would be anything but wonderful. After a full minute of silence Amber reengaged. "Mecca, huh?" The women nodded in agreement. "And where is this quilting utopia?"

"The Missouri Star Quilt Company in Hamilton."

"Never heard of it," Amber said.

"Hamilton or the Missouri Star..." The oldest and the grayest of the women chuckled.

"No, of course you haven't heard of Hamilton. It's just a tiny little town. You'll only find it if you're looking."

Amber considered those words as she slowly chewed her bagel. "So it's pretty remote?"

"A hidden gem," the lady responded.

Amber contemplated deeply as she took another bite. Never in a thousand years would she have considered going to a quilt shop in a tiny Missouri town. But maybe it would be an equally impossible conclusion for her pursuers. Amber swallowed her food and rubbed the stress from her forehead. "I don't suppose you..." She paused.

"What is it dear?"

Amber steeled her determination and then lied...kind of. "Hamilton sounds like a fascinating place. Do you have room for one more?"